TREASURES OF
Nevada

by William Faubion

a part of the Morgan & Chase Treasure Series
www.treasuresof.com

MORGAN & CHASE PUBLISHING INC.

THE TREASURE SERIES

Morgan & Chase Publishing, Inc.
531 Parsons Drive, Medford, Oregon 97501
(888) 557-9328
www.treasuresof.com

Printed and bound by Taylor Specialty Books—Dallas TX
First edition 2007
ISBN: 978-1-933989-16-7

*I gratefully acknowledge the contributions
of the many people involved in the writing and production of this book.
Their tireless dedication to this endeavour has been inspirational.*
—Damon Neal, *Publisher*

The Morgan & Chase Publishing Home Team

Operations Department:
V.P. of Operations—Cindy Tilley Faubion
Travel Writer Liaison—Anne Boydston
Shipping & Receiving—Virginia Arias
Human Resources Coordinator Heather Allen
Customer Service Relations—Casey Faubion, Terrie West, Sue Buda, Marie Manson
IT Engineer—Ray Ackerman
Receptionist—Shauna O'Callahan

Production Department:
Proof Editors—Avery Brown, Clarice Rodriguez, Tiffany Myers
Editor/Writers—Gregory Scott, Robyn Sutherland
House Writer—Megan Glomb
Photo Coordinator—Wendy L. Gay
Photo Assistant—Donna Lindley
Photo Editor—Mary Murdock
Graphic Design Team—C.S. Rowan, Jesse Gifford, Tamara Cornett, Jacob Kristof, Michael Frye

Administrative Department:
CFO—Emily Wilke
Accounting Assistants—Danielle Barkley, David Grundvig, Cari Qualls
Website Designer—Molly Bermea
Website Software Developer—Ben Ford

Contributing Writers:
Mary Beth Lee, Lynda Kusick, Mark Allen Deruiter, Sharon Mills, Sharron Walley, Kathy Johnson, Andre Osborne, Dusty Alexander, Paul Hadella, Mary Knepp, Chris McCrellis-Mitchell, Laura Young, Todd Wels, Jennifer Buckner, Carol Bevis, Amber Dusk, Alexis McKenna, Maggie McClellen, Nancy McClain

Special Recognition to:
Pam Hamilton, David Smigelski, John Gaffey, Chris Rose-Merkle, Gene Mitts

For everyone who loves the opportunity and excitement that Nevada provides.

How to use this book

Treasures of Nevada is divided by region and category. Categories range from accommodations to wines, with headings such as attractions, bakeries, galleries, home, recreation, restaurants and shopping in between.

In the index, all of these Treasures are listed alphabetically by name as well as by the city where you can visit them.

We have provided contact information for every Treasure in the book.
These are places and businesses that we encourage you to visit on your travels through Nevada.

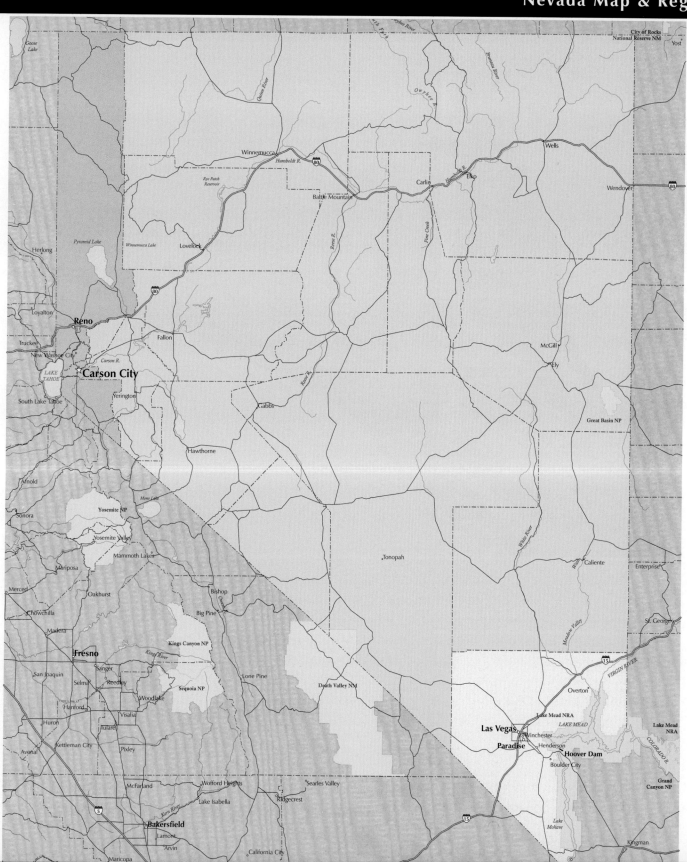

NEVADA FACTS:

Admitted to the Union: 1864, the 36th state   Animal: Desert Bighorn Sheep

OFFICE OF THE GOVERNOR

Greetings from the Governor & First Lady

As Governor of Nevada, it is my pleasure to welcome you to *Treasures of Nevada*. This book is a great resource that can lead you to some of the most intriguing places in the Great State of Nevada.

The Silver State is a jewel in many facets – from its desert landscapes to its towering mountain peaks; from pristine Lake Tahoe to the unparalleled Great Basin National Park; from its rustic small towns to the fastest growing cities in the United States. Nevada is a state steeped in culture, history and diversity.

Nevada is one of the most versatile states in what we have to offer, from world famous gaming establishments and dramatic scenery of the desert, to the man-made wonders of Lake Mead and Hoover Dam. There is the historic mining town of Virginia City, and the City of Lovelock which encompasses the ancient Chinese tradition of symbolically locking one's love.

The Treasures in this book exemplify a spirit of adventure, beauty & hospitality on which we pride ourselves. We invite you to seek them out for yourself.

Sincerely,

Governor Jim Gibbons

First Lady Dawn Gibbons

Foreword

Welcome to *Treasures of Nevada*. This book is a resource that can guide you to some of the best places in the State of Nevada, one of the most vibrant and exciting parts of America. Nevada is a state of contrasts, from the big skies and wide vistas of Greater Nevada to the neon-lit playgrounds of its great cities.

Nevada's history is one of the most distinctive of any state. In 1948, the Mexican-American War made it a United States possession. In 1859, prospectors discovered the Comstock Lode, a rich outcropping of gold and silver. This discovery brought a flood of miners, prospectors, merchants and others hoping to strike it rich. Nevada became a territory in 1861 and a state in 1864 during the Civil War. Its admission was rushed to help re-elect President Abraham Lincoln. In later years, the state's small population created difficulties that the legislature addressed by legalizing activities forbidden in neighboring California, such as casino gambling. The result was the gaming industry and the world-famous resorts of Reno and Las Vegas. Today, Las Vegas has grown into a major metropolis with a vast range of economic activities.

Countless attractions await visitors to Nevada. You can prospect for opals up north or go skydiving down south. See a show or place a wager in the awesome casino hotels on Las Vegas Boulevard or take in a camel race at Virginia City. Go skiing near Lake Tahoe or visit the State Museum in Carson City. You can shop for jewelry in Las Vegas—or even get married to your sweetheart.

Nevada is home to the nicest people you'll ever meet. In preparing this book, we talked to literally thousands of business people about their products, their services and their vision. We visited art galleries in Mesquite and spas in Reno. We stayed at a ranch in Deeth and dined well in Pahrump. You are holding the result of our efforts in your hands. *Treasures of Nevada* is a 215-page compilation of the best places in Nevada to eat, shop, play, explore, learn and relax. We did the legwork. All you have to do now is enjoy.

—Cindy Tilley Faubion

Red Rock Canyon, just west of Las Vegas

Las Vegas Area

Don Laughlin's
Riverside Resort Hotel & Casino

When Don Laughlin opened the doors to his Riverside Resort Hotel & Casino in 1966, he knew that the 12 slot machines and two gaming tables were only a start. In those days, he enticed people to come and play by offering them all-you-can-eat chicken dinners for 98 cents. These days, crowds flock to the town named after this gaming pioneer to experience an entire world of exciting entertainment that he has created. One expansion after another has brought more rooms, more slots, more video poker machines and more tables for card games, roulette and craps. Over the years, Don has added the Race & Sports Book, the Riverside Lanes bowling center and Don's Celebrity Theatre to the mix. You can take a luxury cruise on the Colorado River during the day and party in the dance hall and nightclub in the evening. Restaurants from buffet to gourmet cater to every palate and budget. An RV park features 740 spaces with full hook-up facilities. Don's fascination with gaming began while he was growing up in Minnesota. He bought some mail-order slot machines, installed them in local pubs and was soon making $500 a week. His principal threatened to kick him out of school if he didn't quit the slot machine business, so he quit school instead. After leaving Minnesota, he opened a club in Vegas. The town now called Laughlin was just a patch of desert when he first set eyes on it in 1964. Come to the Riverside Resort Hotel & Casino and see how big Don's dream has grown.

1650 S Casino Drive, Laughlin NV
(702) 298-2535 *www.riversideresort.com*

Boulder Dam Hotel

Hidden away between the glitz of Las Vegas and the colossal wonder of Hoover Dam, you'll find the Boulder Dam Hotel, a gracious Dutch Colonial-style hotel in the heart of historic Boulder City. Built in 1933 to house visiting government and corporate project managers supervising the building of Hoover Dam, the Boulder Dam Hotel quickly became known for the many celebrities who stayed there, including Will Rogers, Bette Davis and Howard Hughes. When World War II broke out, the dam was closed to visitors. Without tourists the hotel struggled to survive but never recovered. In the 1980s, the building was slated to be condemned, but Boulder City residents refused to give up, raising millions of dollars to restore it. Local volunteers performed much of the actual restoration work, and today the hotel again shines as the Grand Dame of Boulder City. It was named to the National Register of Historic Places on August 19, 1982. One room features actual furniture from the 1930s, and the entire structure gives visitors and guests a feel for what life was like then. The Boulder City/Hoover Dam Museum is housed in the hotel, and its interactive displays and exhibits tell the extraordinary stories of those who faced the complexity and dangers of building Hoover Dam and Boulder City. Visit the Boulder Dam Hotel and Museum for a fascinating look at the hospitality and history of a bygone era.

1305 Arizona Street, Boulder City NV
(702) 293-3510 *www.boulderdamhotel.com*

Holiday Inn Express
Hotel & Suites West (The Lakes)

Combining upscale accommodations with outstanding service, the Holiday Inn Express Hotel & Suites West, known as The Lakes, delights families as well as business travelers. General Manager Grace Robinson and Assistant Manager Marjorie Darnell bring more than 23 years of international experience to the establishment, and the friendly, attentive staff offers a warm smile and first class service to every guest. Located across from Canyon Gate Golf Course and Country Club, the boutique style hotel is within walking distance of shopping and fine restaurants and offers easy access to the Las Vegas Strip and Red Rock Canyon. The newly renovated facility features guest accommodations in every size to serve the needs of business, government and vacationing guests. Some suites offer kitchens and spas. Broadband Internet access and luxurious granite countertops in the baths complete each tastefully decorated room. The hotel restaurant offers everything from fast food to fine dining and serves a free breakfast in the morning. The hotel is one of three Las Vegas Holiday Inn Express hotels owned by the Fine Hospitality Group. For spacious, updated rooms, first-rate amenities and gracious service, discover the Holiday Inn Express Hotel & Suites West on your next Las Vegas trip.

8669 W Sahara Avenue, Las Vegas NV (West) (702) 256-3766
4035 N Nellis Boulevard, Las Vegas NV (Nellis) (702) 644-5700
4540 Donovan Way, North Las Vegas NV (North) (702) 649-3000
www.finehospitality.com

Bonnie Springs Old Nevada

Bonnie Springs Ranch was built in 1843 as a stopover for wagon trains heading to California on the Old Spanish Trail. Today it is one of the Las Vegas area's finest family attractions. In 1950 Al Levinson arrived in Las Vegas from New York. He soon fell in love with Bonnie McGaugh, a Las Vegas showgirl. Al and Bonnie married, and with a shared passion for the West, they decided to recreate and preserve as much of Old Nevada as they could. The result is Bonnie Springs Old Nevada, a replica of an 1880s mining town built on the 115-acre Bonnie Springs Ranch. There is plenty of action in this old town, where wooden sidewalks creak under your feet as tumbleweeds blow by. Kids can help a posse chase a bad guy, and maybe witness a public hanging. Cowboys and Cowgirls are everywhere, along with miniature train rides, a petting zoo, and a wax museum. Old Nevada wouldn't be complete without a large stable of horses for your riding pleasure. Enjoy a ride through the Red Rock Canyon. Shop for turquoise, silver and other Western souvenirs. Enjoy great homemade meals at the restaurant, hit the lounge, and spend the night. Themed rooms are available, with fireplaces and love tubs or kitchen suites. Bonnie Springs Old Nevada is even equipped with a beautiful 1800s-style chapel. It is a great place to get swept off your feet. If you want to experience a piece of the Old West, head to Bonnie Springs. It's a fun place you'll never forget.

1 Gunfighter Lane, Blue Diamond NV
(702) 875-4191
www.bonniesprings.com

Flea Bag's Barkery & Bow-tique

If you're looking for ways to indulge your furry best friend, check out Flea Bag's Barkery & Bow-tique in The District at Green Valley Ranch. This upscale barkery bakes fresh treats daily and offers specialty goods for treasured pets as well. Owner Vicki LePore, a Las Vegas native, worked in the casino industry for 25 years before starting her own business in 2001. A dog lover since childhood, Vicki's own Jack Russell terrier, Ally, is the dog on the store's logo. Her customers are special to her, and she knows many of her regulars by their first names, and their humans too. Flea Bag's celebrates the Saturday before Halloween with Doggie Howl & Whine, an annual event that includes a dog costume contest. The barkery offers healthy treats made with whole wheat flour, wheat germ, canola oil and chicken and beef broth, and goodies include bone-shaped pizzas and carob treats that are safer for dogs than chocolate. If your pooch is panting for a personalized bowl, a leopard skin collar or a cushy carrier, you'll find it here. Pets of the feline persuasion will also find toys with catnip, fancy collars and harnesses. Check out the shop's oil pastel pet portraits, done by Vicki's daughter, Whitney LePore-Leach. Whether you're looking for stylish pet accessories, treats or a birthday cake for your faithful friend, you'll find it at Flea Bag's Barkery & Bow-tique.

2225 Village Walk Drive, Suite 173, Henderson NV
(702) 914-8805
www.fleabagsonline.com

Portraits by Catherine

Catherine, a certified professional photographer, is well known for her portraiture of children, families, graduates and pets. All sessions are by appointment only, giving you time to relax and enjoy your portrait experience. Her Enchanted Children Series puts your child in magical scenes. These scenes range from fairies, angels and mermaids to western, gone fishin' and vintage baseball. Scenes for pets are equally well thought out. The resulting portraits are artistically rendered with precision and skill and are some of the most beautiful you will ever see. You may even see your previews the same day as your session. The studio is completely digital, which means more creativity and fun. The studio is also one of the largest and best equipped in the Las Vegas Valley, accommodating groups of up to twenty-five people. Catherine Guillotte grew up with a photographer father and her work reveals an expert eye and captivating personal style. Visit Portraits by Catherine and bring home a lasting memory. All of her portraits are professionally crafted and personally guaranteed.

2300 N Rainbow Boulevard, #111, Las Vegas NV
(702) 432-3103
www.portraitsbycatherine.com

Snooty Pets

Snooty Pets in Las Vegas gives you plenty of ways to pamper your four-legged family members with the finest food, clothing, bakery goodies and grooming services. Enhancing the Lives of Pets is more than a motto to owners Stephanie and Kevin Thomas, it's their whole mission. They work hard to find items for your pets that are not offered in other stores. They make their delicious pet bakery goodies right in the store. Consider a peanut butter birthday cake in honor of your dog's special day. Treat your favorite feline to the scrumptious cat cuisine and treats found here. You will also find plenty of clothes that will have your pooch fashionable year-round, with T-shirts, sweaters and coats. The store also carries walking harnesses, leashes and one-of-a-kind identification tags. Snooty Pets grooming salon offers services ranging from bath and scissor finishing to relaxing massage and mud bath treatments. If you're really looking to give your pet the ultimate experience, try one of the Snooty Spa Packages. To offer your pet the best in clothes, treats, food and grooming services, head to Snooty Pets.

8560 W Desert Inn, Suite D-4, Las Vegas NV
(corner of Desert Inn and Durango, in front of Vons)
(702) 396-5510
www.snootypets.com

Lush Puppy

When was the last time you treated your pup to a polka-dot rain slicker or a pearl necklace? At Lush Puppy, you can lavish your beloved mutt with every luxury, from clothing and collars to treats, toys and bath products. Owners Roe Astuto and Farrel Freeman opened the store in 2005 inside the Mandalay Place mall, a part of the Mandalay Bay Resort & Casino. Roe is a former marketing and advertising vice president, while Farrel is a successful clothing and floral designer with an eye for style. "We try to offer fashion and accessories that one wouldn't find in a big retailer," Roe says. You'll find bomber vests, tank tops and trench coats here. Styles range from pink poodle elegance to pound hound charming, with lines from such well-known designers as Juicy Couture and Donald Pliner. You can dress up Fido in fancy footwear or let him nibble on a pair of Jimmy Chew shoes, a soft bottle of Dog Perignon or a Chewy Vuiton plush handbag. Perhaps it's time to gift your pooch with a red Furrari car bed. Lush Puppy pampers cats, too. Isn't your feline due for some Kitty Kaviar and swanky bowl or a chenille blanket of his very own? The mall and the shop welcome pets on leashes, so why not bring them along to help out with the shopping fun? For posh choices for your pet, visit Lush Puppy.

Mandalay Place, 3930 Las Vegas Boulevard S, Las Vegas NV
(702) 740-2254
www.lushpuppyonline.com

Acrylic Tank Manufacturing

Acrylic Tank Manufacturing in Las Vegas can create a custom aquarium for your home or commercial exhibits and underwater viewing panels for zoos, museums and public aquariums. Owners Wayde King and Brett Raymer, along with their staff, have a combined 100 years of experience with aquariums. They will come to you, no matter where you are, to do preliminary interviews and take a look at your space before beginning the design process. The service doesn't stop after their installation, either. They will maintain their creation and will even service the designs of others. From 50 to 50,000 gallons, the Acrylic Tank team can create any design you bring to them. They can also start from scratch to design a life support system, custom coral creations and cabinetry in nearly any shape you might need. An Acrylic Tank aquarium makes a fascinating piece of living art for your restaurant, bar or office. A tour of the plant and showroom offers opportunities to see current projects; you can also take home an interactive CD to learn more. Acrylic Tank has built aquariums for T-REX Theme Park, the PALMS Hotel Casino and magician David Blaine. The company also sells fish, food and basic items to fill and maintain your tank. To understand what makes Acrylic Tank Manufacturing a world leader in custom aquariums, stop by for a visit.

6125 Annie Oakley Drive, Las Vegas NV
(702) 387-2016 *www.acrylicaquariums.com*

Scrappy-Do
& Other Stuff, Too

Scrappy-Do & Other Stuff, Too offers scrapbookers everything they'll need to create keepsakes of their most precious moments. "You're preserving your memories," says owner Misti Corbett, whose love of scrapbooking is evident throughout the Henderson store. Here, scrappers find an abundance of specialty tools, including eyelets, hole punches and other essentials. You will find pages for your scrapbook in many colors and eye-pleasing designs to mark your most special occasions. Scrappy-Do stocks other stuff, too, including craft supplies, gifts and candles. "Scrappy-Do has more of a community feeling," says Misti, explaining what sets her store apart from other craft shops. You'll often find customers working together in the store's classroom. Among the opportunities to learn and socialize are the special Scrappy-Time events, when customers can put together their scrapbooks with help from Scrappy-Do's instructors. Scrappy-Time also features games, prizes and giveaways. The store holds a page of the month event that shows off the creativity of its customers. In addition, Scrappy-Do hosts bridal showers, birthday parties and other special events. Misti's sense of community extends to a program she has developed for the area's schools. For scrapbooking that understands your heart, visit Scrappy-Do & Other Stuff, Too.

1550 W Horizon Ridge Parkway, Suite R, Henderson NV
(702) 407-5589
www.scrappy-do.com

Quiltique

The bright and contemporary Quiltique in Henderson is an exciting destination for anyone who loves to quilt, sew, stitch, or would like to learn. Great classes and stock that changes regularly keep customers always coming back. The cheerful staff is one of the highlights of a trip to Quiltique. Owners Bob and Jan Tibesar and their daughters, Kara Tibesar and Jennifer Albaugh welcome your questions and willingness to learn. Jan has been a quilter for years, so turning her hobby into a successful business was a natural step. The shop carries over 5,000 bolts of cloth at any one time, and the store's lighting is designed to highlight the beautiful fabrics. You will especially find fabric for non-traditional quilts that require unusual prints and colors, plus a great selection of juvenile and novelty fabrics. Quiltique is also a great place to find books, kits, notions, machine embroidery supplies, and software for all your sewing and quilting needs. If you are looking for a sewing machine, they are a Bernina Authorized Dealership and carry top of the line machines and accessories. If you are not quite ready to quilt or sew on your own, or just want to hone in on your skills, the staff offers classes for all skill levels. Quilting may be a traditional craft, but it has also found many ways to become part of a modern age. "People get inspired by the more contemporary quilt designs we offer. There is a whole new generation out there with a strong desire to be part of something from the past, but to make it something new," says Jennifer. When you have an itch to stitch, start with a visit to Quiltique.

213 N Stephanie Street, Suite E, Henderson NV (702) 563-8600
www.quiltique.com

Kessler & Sons Music

Chuck Kessler would love to work on your musical instrument to get it playing right. He opened his business in 1989 after a stint doing repairs at somebody else's music shop. Hoping to make a living as an instrument doctor, he soon found that what he could provide Las Vegas went far beyond effective and honest repairs. Today Kessler & Sons Music has three locations offering sales, rentals and lessons. Although Chuck's business has grown beyond his expectations, repairs bring him back to his roots and remain an important part of his services. The stores rent thousands of instruments to parents in the area. Band and orchestra instruments are the specialty. "We don't sell pianos and organs, but everything else," says Chuck, who is joined by his wife, Becky, and son David in running the business. That "everything else" includes flutes and trumpets as well as cellos, violins and guitars. Perhaps your prodigious child excels at the clarinet and is hinting that she would like to try the bassoon. Kessler & Sons Music is the place to take her. You can also shop at the company's Internet site. When you call to order, you are always going to speak to either Chuck or Dave, not just some phone operator in a call center. "That's the main thing that sets us apart," says Chuck. "We're very customer friendly." Come to Kessler & Sons Music to make your life more musical.

3047 E Charleston Boulevard, Las Vegas NV (702) 385-BAND (2263)
2350 S Rainbow Boulevard, Suite 8, Las Vegas NV (702) 242-2263
8866 S Eastern Avenue, Suite 100, Las Vegas NV (702) 492-7263
www.kesslermusic.com

Vegas Beads

At Vegas Beads, customers discover 2,600 square feet brimming with beads of every size, shape and color. Owners Tim and Tom decided to forego corporate America and move from Seattle to Las Vegas to start the shop. They envisioned a roomy store large enough to really see and appreciate a fascinating variety of beads and also focused on making the bead shopping experience fun and affordable. Vegas Beads, which opened in 2004, provides a comfortable environment where families are welcome. Customers appreciate the service provided by friendly staff members who eagerly share their expertise and knowledge. Want to stretch your creative side? Vegas Beads offers jewelry making classes for beginners and more advanced hobbyists. You can learn about the ins and outs of wire wrapping or beading bracelets, earrings and necklaces. Customers can craft seasonal items, such as Christmas pins and Thanksgiving turkey earrings; they can also learn the right angle weave using Swarovski crystals. Tim and Tom sponsor residents of New Vista, a center for mentally challenged adults, by providing small work projects for the residents and paying them well for their efforts. A schedule of classes and product ordering is available online, but if you are in Las Vegas, you will want to come in to the store to check out all the variety and family fun for yourself.

3480 Spring Mountain Road, Las Vegas NV
(702) 452-3237
www.vegasbeads.com

The Artful Potter

The Artful Potter offers a paint-your-own pottery studio as well as what owner Elizabeth Le calls art therapy. For nearly 10 years, customers have been selecting delightful items to paint, then creating personal treasures in a colorful environment designed to enhance the imagination. You paint it, and the Artful Potter will glaze and fire it for you. Bring your children and make a precious keepsake out of their tiny handprints or footprints. Come in next year and see how they've grown. Kids and parents enjoy working on projects together. Paints are water-based and nontoxic; the glazes are safe for food. Paint Me a Story is a popular program, offering story time for children and a corresponding ceramic piece to paint. The Artful Potter is a splendid place to bring your friends for a fun birthday gathering, a bridal or baby shower. A corporate gathering here makes a nice break from the office and a chance for everyone to relax and share a creative experience. "The pottery experience is like capturing a moment in time," says Elizabeth, who has always been a fan of contemporary ceramics. The studio offers 600 different pieces ready for you to paint, in addition to stamps, stencils and idea books to help you with your masterpiece. The staff is always available to answer questions, and finished projects can be picked up a few days after your session. Find your inner artist at the Artful Potter.

2351 N Rainbow, Suite 102, Las Vegas NV (702) 638-1775
8826 S Eastern Avenue, Suite 114, Las Vegas NV (702) 966-6300
www.artfulpotter.com

Water Street District

The Water Street District, situated in the original downtown section of Henderson, is enjoying a rebirth as a pedestrian-friendly, centrally located magnet for shopping, working, living and entertainment. When Henderson burgeoned in the 1950s, the Water Street District was at its hub, but suffered neglect in more recent years. The revitalization of Henderson's core helps the city retain its friendly, small-town feel despite its closeness to Las Vegas. "This is not the Strip. We're relaxed, social and family oriented," says Michelle Romero, Henderson's redevelopment project manager. By encouraging public partnering with the private sector, the Water Street District is attracting great restaurants, galleries and boutiques. The Pinnacle, designed and constructed almost entirely by a woman entrepreneur, offers executive suites and attractive amenities. It also houses a restaurant on the first floor. Water Street South adds still more public and private enterprise to the area as home to the Nevada State College Nursing Program, Mojo Bean Coffee House, Clark County Credit Union and other businesses. The project has created such a demand for office space that they recently completed construction of phase two. The Water Street District is an enjoyable destination for families, thanks to the Events Plaza, which hosts art exhibitions, classic car shows and other special events. Discover the revitalized core of Henderson with a visit to the Water Street District.

240 Water Street, Henderson NV
(702) 267-1516
www.waterstreetdistrict.com

Las Vegas Natural History Museum

Las Vegas isn't just for grownups these days, thanks to an influx of child-friendly attractions like the Las Vegas Natural History Museum. This private, nonprofit museum gives youngsters the opportunity to explore the world around them through interactive exhibits, educational programs and collections. The museum endeavors to instill an appreciation and understanding of our world's wildlife and ecosystems while exploring the relationship between humans and the environment. Watch animated dinosaurs, then explore the watery depths of the ocean to see how live sharks and other marine animals live. Still another area of the museum houses live snakes and lizards. At the Young Scientist's Center, children can dig for fossils and check out a paleontologist's lab. In an effort to keep things fresh, the museum organizes a full range of exhibits and special events and has devised such programs as the weekly Saturday science projects and an annual traveling exhibit. See another side of this glamorous city in the desert with a visit to the Las Vegas Natural History Museum.

900 Las Vegas Boulevard, Las Vegas NV
(702) 384-3466
www.Lvnhm.org

Atomic Testing Museum

If you've been searching for an explosive vacation attraction that is anything but ordinary, then fire up your brain and head to the Atomic Testing Museum. The Atomic Testing Museum is a program of the Nevada Test Site Historical Foundation, or NTSHF, and is dedicated to educating the public about atomic testing, nuclear weapons and Cold War history as well as offering information about the Nevada Test Site itself. Museum Director Bill Johnson and Troy Wade, NTSHF president, recognize the controversy surrounding the history of nuclear weaponry and welcome advocates both for and against the practice. The Atomic Testing Museum explains events leading up to the establishment of the test site and describes the progression of above and underground testing performed there. In the Ground Zero Theater visitors experience a simulation of an aboveground test followed by a nine-minute narrative that reflects upon the history of atomic testing. The museum also features a replica of the Control Point, the spot where the countdown took place prior to each test. A variety of exhibits pass through the Harry Reid Exhibit Hall. Be sure to stop by the museum store, where movies, gifts and memorabilia from the Atomic Age line the shelves, each piece a souvenir of the memorable excursion awaiting you at the Atomic Testing Museum.

755 E Flamingo Road, Las Vegas NV
(702) 794-5161
www.atomictestingmuseum.org

The Liberace Foundation and Museum

No trip to Las Vegas would be complete without a visit to the Liberace Museum, which pays homage to Mr. Showmanship himself. The museum, opened in 1979, is possible thanks to the support of the Liberace Foundation. In 1976, Liberace himself founded the nonprofit foundation to grant scholarships to performing arts students. To date, the foundation has awarded more than $5 million in scholarships to some 2,200 students in 100 universities. The performer's life goal was to be known as a "kind and generous soul," a tradition that lives on within the foundation through current Executive Director R. Darin Hollingsworth, who has a great love for the performing arts and a commitment to keeping Liberace's dream alive. Up until the 1980s, Liberace was the highest paid entertainer in Las Vegas, regularly selling out shows to fans who delighted in watching him perform in flamboyant costumes, which sometimes weighed as much as 200 pounds. You'll see elaborate capes and jumpsuits designed by Liberace's fourth and final costume designer Michael Travis here and furs created by Anna Nateece. Beyond dazzling costumes, visitors enjoy Liberace's glitzy pianos, jewelry and automobiles. A museum store offers tapes and music related items as well as tickets to tribute concerts. Join fans from all over the world who come to the Liberace Museum to pay tribute to one of the most fascinating entertainers of our time.

1775 E Tropicana Avenue, Las Vegas NV (702) 798-5595 *www.liberace.org*

Sundance Helicopters

Sundance Helicopters has been voted the Best Helicopter Company in Nevada five years in a row by *Nevada Magazine*, and it is not a surprise. Sundance Helicopters offers the best assortment of amazing sightseeing packages available in the Las Vegas area. Their most popular packages involve flights over and through the Grand Canyon, but they offer a dizzying array of options, from champagne flights to gourmet dinner flights covering all of the area's top destinations, including the Las Vegas Strip. Sundance Helicopters began in 1985 as a flight-training company operating out of Sky Harbor Airport. The company expanded to provide military support, firefighting, traffic reporting and power line surveys, and eventually moved to McCarran International Airport. Tourism, especially tours of the Grand Canyon, became the largest part of the company's operation. Sundance still devotes up to four helicopters every summer for firefighting, and major Hollywood production companies, such as Warner Brothers, Paramount and Disney, utilize its expertise for film projects. But sightseeing has made Sundance the best-known helicopter company in Nevada. Sundance is also known for its civic contributions, donating generously to charitable and non-profit organizations such as the Make-A-Wish Foundation. During the Holidays, Santa often arrives on a Sundance helicopter to greet groups of children. The next time you visit Las Vegas, make reservations to fly with the best there is. Sundance Helicopters will provide an experience that is far beyond your expectations.

5596 Haven Street, Las Vegas NV
(702) 736-0606 or (800) 653-1881
www.sundancehelicopters.com

Lake Mead Cruises

Take a journey aboard the sternwheeler, *Desert Princess,* and view Lake Mead from an entirely different perspective. Lake Mead is 110 miles long and the *Desert Princess* rolls along at about seven miles per hour. This is a very special way to see Hoover Dam. Listen to the history of the dam and Lake Mead as you marvel at the natural wonders. Enjoy the scenic beauty of Black Canyon, where the mountain colors vary from granite to crimson. There is a good chance you will spot Big Horn Sheep as they browse on the sheer cliffs. Watch coyotes hunt and play. This is a different view of Las Vegas. A little more relaxed, no neon lights. Lake Mead Cruises has been offering its unrivaled cruises since 1991. There are mid-day sight-seeing cruises, Dinner Cruises, Dinner & Dance Cruises, Pizza Party Cruises and Champagne Brunch Cruises. You can ride on either the *Desert Princess* or her little sister, the *Desert Princess Too*. Whatever you choose, you'll know you made the right decision. Lake Mead Cruises won the *Zagat* award for Best Champagne Brunch and most intimate weddings. They are recipients of the Governor's Tourism Development Award. They know a thing or two about service. They keep a full grill on board for all the sightseeing tours. There's a snack bar and a full service beverage bar that's always open. Boarding photos are available for optional purchase when you return to dock. It's best to call ahead and reserve your place, as space is limited. Give your next visit to Las Vegas a new perspective with Lake Mead Cruises.

490 B Horsepower Cove, Boulder City NV
(702) 293-6180
www.lakemeadcruises.com

Classical Entertainment, Inc.

Classical Entertainment offers upscale musical entertainment for corporate functions, private parties, weddings and other special events in and around Las Vegas. Cynthia Harris, a freelance pianist and music educator in the Las Vegas Valley since the early 1980s, formed Classical Entertainment in 2003 in response to a need for a high quality product coupled with integrity in service. With a performance background in classical music, Harris is a music broker and music consultant who supplies the client with the finest live music the Las Vegas Valley has to offer—from soloists, duos and trios to small ensembles, jazz combos, big bands and chamber ensembles. Classical Entertainment also has singers, dancers, impersonators, magicians, costumed musicians, and can supply the client with all types of world music. Classical Entertainment has booked musical entertainment into the major upscale properties, including the Venetian, Caesar's Palace, Wynn, JW Marriott, Lake Las Vegas and many others. In addition to running Classical Entertainment, Harris plays weekly at the Stirling Club at Turnberry and serves as Artistic Director of the Performing Arts Program at the Andre Agassi College Preparatory Academy. For your next corporate event or private function, call Classical Entertainment for music customized for your tastes.

7380 S Eastern Avenue, Suite 124-307, Las Vegas NV
(702) 558-2973
www.classicalentertainment.com

Laughter Unlimited

Finely prepared dinners, decadent desserts and dead bodies at table four are all part of the fun at Laughter Unlimited, where owner Eric Post and his mischievous troupe of actors plot, plan and provide plenty of giggles for their unsuspecting guests. Eric founded this interactive dinner theater in 1997 and has since been bringing laughs galore to enchanted audiences who get to guess who done it while dining on scrumptious dinner entrées, such as the No Bull steak plate, featuring aged Black Angus beef, or Something Fishy, a delicious eight-ounce grilled salmon steak topped with a creamy lemon and dill cheese sauce. Prior to launching his own theater business, Eric served as a Navy pilot and earned a Bachelor of Fine Arts degree from the California Institute of the Arts. He got a feel for the dinner theater scene while working in one of Las Vegas' major casinos. Since going out on his own, he has successfully gained a reputation for putting on a sensational show. Laughter Unlimited features the award winning comedy *Marriage Can Be Murder*. Expect hijinks galore as guests become intermingled with cast members and are then called upon to become a part of the performance, right alongside the villains and victims. Enjoy an affordable and laugh-filled evening that's to die for at Laughter Unlimited.

4533 W Sahara, Las Vegas NV
(702) 616-3322
www.marriagecanbemurder.com

Aerobatic Experience

Craig Fordem says, "people come to Las Vegas to have the thrill of a lifetime," and at Aerobatic Experience, just 30 minutes from the Strip at the Boulder City airport, he delivers both a scenic ride and the adrenalin rush of a screaming airborne roller coaster. Craig, owner and aerobatic ace, lets you experience the exciting maneuvers usually reserved solely for air show and fighter pilots: rolls, loops, hammerhead turns and inverted flight. Craig has been involved in aerobatic flying for 40 years and also teaches specialized flight training, educating pilots on flying at unusual attitudes. He leads training with the Chilean Air Force a couple of times a year in Boulder City, and has also worked with the United States Navy. His unique aircraft is the Extra 300/L, the Ferrari of all aerobatic planes, and the only two-seat aircraft of its kind that's certified by the FAA for 10 Gs in the United States. Flown by aerobatic competitors and air show performers throughout the world, the aircraft has 300 horsepower and a roll rate of over 400 degrees per second. If that sounds a bit over-the-top for your taste, you can opt for the more leisurely tour of awe-inspiring Hoover Dam. A video of your ride is available, too. If you've never seen the Colorado River upside-down, this is your chance. Come be a part of Craig's exquisitely heart-pounding aerial ballet at Aerobatic Experience.

61B Boulder City Airport, Boulder City NV
(702) 985-0600
www.aerobaticexperience.com

Heli USA

In how many languages have the helicopter pilots at Heli USA heard the words *awesome* and *mind-blowing*? Flights bound for the Grand Canyon leave from McCarran Airport in Las Vegas with passengers from all over the world. A travel writer for the *Irish Daily Mirror* loved his aerial tour of American's greatest natural attraction. "Flying low through the massive split in the earth in a cloudless sky is an unbelievable experience," he told the folks back home. "I will never forget the helicopter soaring over the western rim of the canyon and the sheer immensity of this natural wonder hitting me smack between the eyes." For even more adventure, you could combine your flight with a stay at the Grand Canyon West Ranch, where horseback riding, dinner and a cowboy sing-along are part of the fun. Another popular Heli USA tour takes passengers over the Las Vegas Strip at night. Indeed, variety is one thing that sets Heli USA apart. Another is experience. Heli USA proudly flew its one millionth passenger in 2007. Its pilots meet the same standards as those of the major airlines, while strictly adhering to the company's policies of safe altitudes and no sharp banking. Remember Heli USA when you are in Oahu and Kauai, too, for tours that you'll want to talk about to everyone back home.

235 E Tropicana Avenue, Las Vegas NV
(702) 736-8787 or (800) 359-8727
www.heliusa.com

Yoomi Lee (Sugar Plum Fairy) and Kyudong Kwak (Cavileer)
Bruce Steivel's *Nutcracker*, 2006
Photo by John Hanson

Bruce Steivel's *Vegas the Early Years,* 2005
Photo by Edyta Sokolowska

Bruce Steivel's *Dracula,* 2006
Photo by Edyta Sokolowska

Nevada Ballet Theatre

Las Vegas is home to the state's largest professional ballet company, the award-winning Nevada Ballet Theatre (NBT). You will love its repertoire, which includes popular story ballets each season, such as *Peter Pan*, *Cinderella* or *Romeo and Juliet* as well as cutting-edge pieces from the greatest as well as emerging choreographers. About 38 dancers with international performing experience take to the stage for five core productions each season under the direction of Bruce Steivel, Artistic Director. The company's annual *Nutcracker,* in December, is a holiday favorite for thousands of residents and tourists alike. The dancers are classically trained, in keeping with the concepts on which NBT was founded in 1972. The expectations of today's audiences also require great versatility, and NBT interprets contemporary scores with heart-wrenching pathos and soaring grace. NBT enriches the cultural landscape of Las Vegas with community and educational programs beyond its performances, and its Academy is the only dance school affiliated with a professional ballet company in the state of Nevada. As NBT looks forward to its next 35 years, its goal remains: to leave audiences emotionally stirred by an extraordinary experience. Join the crowd in a standing ovation at the end of a performance by Nevada Ballet Theatre.

1651 Inner Circle, Las Vegas NV
(702) 24-DANCE (243-2623)
www.nevadaballet.com

Little Pastry Chefs

The folks at Little Pastry Chefs invite you to get in on the action of a bakery kitchen. They bake the cake and then supply you with the design techniques and the tools you need to decorate it like a pro. Cake decorating is not the only do-it-yourself activity that you can try at Little Pastry Chefs. You can also make your own cookies at the cookie bar. Kids and adults of all ages are welcome. The dessert artists at Little Pastry Chefs will also create a cake for you, even if it doesn't stick to a standard rectangular or round shape. In fact, they hope that it doesn't, because they pride themselves on being able to draw, sculpt or build any design that you can imagine. They offer a variety of flavors, fillings and frostings. You supply the idea. Do you need a cake for your team that looks like a basketball hoop? No problem. Little Pastry Chefs also offers instructional classes at its facility. Here is an opportunity for the whole family, including the little ones, to have fun together while learning the basics of baking and decorating. By the end of the session, you will be tasting what you made and bringing the rest home to share the next day. Whether your middle name is I Can Do It or I Need Help, let Little Pastry Chefs be your bakery and entertainment place for the whole family.

7290 W Azure Drive, Las Vegas NV
(702) 869-2922
www.littlepastrychefs.com

Photos © 2006 Chiemi Floyd Photography

Treasured Times Teahouse

Darjeeling, Earl Grey and Chamomile are not only teas but the names of rooms at the Treasured Times Teahouse, where friends and families can gather and create special memories. With its Victorian-style antiques, Treasured Times Teahouse harkens back to a less hectic era, when people gathered every afternoon to pass a few moments in each other's civil company. Owner Cindy Bezard points out that the atmosphere at her charming teahouse almost forces guests to slow down. "There are no to-go cups here," she says, "only fine china teacups that clink with the stirring of the spoon. It's a sound that is quite relaxing." The staff at Treasured Times serves afternoon tea alone, with sweet treats or with a light lunch. Elmwood Inn Fine Teas provides the many varieties, which are available by the cup or pot. The rooms at the teahouse can accommodate up to 14 people and may be reserved for bridal showers, birthdays or other special events. A backyard gazebo, also available by reservation, features a fountain and flowerbed. For calm in the middle of your busy day, visit Treasured Times Teahouse in the Old Town Business District of Boulder City.

550 California Avenue, Boulder City NV (702) 293-6369
www.treasuredtimesteahouse.com

Photos by Brad Appleby/applebyarts.com

Leopold's Bakery

Nothing upstages the bride at a wedding, but Leopold LeBerger's wedding cakes have come close. During a 50-year career in baking that began in Belgium when he was 13, Leopold has worked as the executive pastry chef in such major Las Vegas hotels as the Stardust and Rio. His wedding and other specialty cakes have been much in demand since he, his son Tony and daughter-in-law Michelle opened Leopold's Bakery in 2001. To plan for your special occasion, drop by and view the many cakes on display. Leopold's offers more than 50 different cakes on a regular basis, along with a large selection of exquisite pastries. All are defined by a European flair. You may order single pastries at the bakery or cake by the slice. The tiramisu is especially good. In fact, the tiramisu that you had for dessert last night at that nice restaurant may have come from Leopold's. The folks at this bakery stay focused on what they do best—cakes and pastries. Don't be shy about asking questions, because they enjoy sharing their love for baking with their customers. For cakes and pastries that make any occasion special, try Leopold's Bakery.

10260 W Charleston Boulevard, Suite 4, Las Vegas NV
(702) 407-8686
www.leopoldsbakery.com

Bonjour Euro Bakers

Lovers of authentic European pastries and baked goods will find *amour* at Bonjour Euro Bakers. "We even have the accents," says Chef Stephane, who opened the Las Vegas bakery in 2005 with his partner, Gerard. Staphane and Gerard worked in hotels and bakeries in the south of France for 10 years before coming to America. After a stay in Miami, the two moved to Las Vegas and operated several bakeries here before opening up Bonjour. Stephane's specialty is bread, and the bakery is particularly well known for its crunchy, authentic French baguette. The assortment of breads here includes flaky croissants, olive loaves and strong rye bread. Gerard's specialty is desserts, and few can resist his fruit tarts, cream puffs and mousse. "We use fresh and real ingredients, nothing artificial," says Stephane. Bonjour also serves sandwiches and salads, along with freshly made French fries and delicious coffee drinks. These bakers enjoy creating custom cakes that can add beauty and flavor to a wedding or other special occasion. Families adore the friendly atmosphere as well as the selections here. Indulge in the pleasures of European pastries and handcrafted breads with a visit to Bonjour Euro Bakers. You'll be shouting *c'est magnifique.*

4012 S Rainbow Boulevard, Suite J, Las Vegas NV
(702) 889-0611

Nothing Bundt Cakes

Dena Tripp and Debbie Shwetz do one thing extremely well and stick to it. Their specialty is bundt cakes, those coveted round cakes with a hole in the middle. Each cake celebrates a special moment or occasion and captures the warm memories of yesterday with the fresh approach of today. This concept allows these luscious cakes to be decorated with a lovely silk flower or ribbons, clever messages and personalized message cards that celebrate your special occasion. What a lovely addition one of these cakes would make to your next party or gathering. Companies use them as gifts and for employee and customer recognition. Known for being extremely moist, the bundt cakes at Nothing Bundt Cakes come in three sizes, including the individual-sized Bundtlets. Dena and Debbie bake the cakes fresh each day and offer 10 flavors, including white chocolate raspberry, chocolate-chocolate chip and pecan praline. Velvety cream cheese and butter icing cascades down the sides of each cake, adding that nostalgic taste of home. Dena and Debbie, friends for close to 20 years, made 53 cakes the first Christmas they were in business. They now sell thousands every holiday season and hundreds every day. You can find Nothing Bundt Cakes at two convenient Las Vegas locations. For a cake that is nothing bundt delicious, try Nothing Bundt Cakes.

9711 S Eastern Avenue, Las Vegas NV (702) 314-0520
8512 W Sahara Avenue, Las Vegas NV (702) 871-6301
www.nothingbundtcakes.com

Chocolate Swan

The joy that you feel upon entering the dessert heaven known as the Chocolate Swan is tinged with sadness when you realize that you couldn't possibly try every pretty thing in the display cases. However, this shouldn't stop you from visiting, because isn't one serving of ecstasy better than none at all? Many loyal customers who consider the Chocolate Swan the best dessert place on the Las Vegas Strip go straight to the Death by Chocolate Cake to make their case. A slice of it puts you in touch with four layers of devil's food cake and three layers of chocolate Vienna cream, frosted with a classic French chocolate butter cream. Yes, chocolate is worshipped here. The Chocolate Swan has been a family owned business since 1983. Owner Mary Basta estimates that, since opening, she has made 18 tons of chocolate for use in everything from her cakes and pies to her éclairs, handmade chocolates and truffles. You will also find plenty of desserts that don't feature chocolate, such as key lime pie, frozen custard ice cream and fruit tarts. The only problem is choosing one from the array of temptations vying to be yours. The Chocolate Swan has become the Las Vegas destination for exquisite wedding cakes, custom corporate gifts and specialty cakes. Of course, if you are fortunate enough to discover the Chocolate Swan at the beginning of your stay in Las Vegas, you can always come back tomorrow. Then again, you could move here. For desserts that could make you consider doing just that, drop by the Chocolate Swan.

3930 Las Vegas Boulevard S, Suite 121B, Las Vegas NV
(702) 632-9366
www.chocolateswan.com

The Cupcakery

The Cupcakery is a joyful bakery full of dazzling little cakes that will make your head spin. It's a little boutique packed with yummy goodness that brings out the kid in all of us. These are not ordinary cupcakes. These are some of the best cakes you have ever seen or tasted. The Cupcakery is the brainchild of three former Golden Nugget executive assistants who one day found themselves flipping through a *Food & Wine* magazine, where they read about a cupcake bakery in San Francisco. Six months later, Dawn Kalman, Pamela Faye Jenkins and Laura Santo Pietro opened the Cupcakery, with the slogan, The Best Little Cupcakes in Vegas. These women mean what they say. They use only the finest ingredients to create these miniature pieces of edible art. By their second week in business they were selling out daily by 3 pm. The Boston Dream is a moist vanilla cake with Bavarian cream filling with a cap of chocolate ganache. Oh My Gosh – Ganache! is a luscious marble cake with a chocolate ganache filling and topped with vanilla and chocolate butter cream. Grasshopper is a rich chocolate cake with chocolate mint butter cream frosting. They even make a cinnamon swirl Good Morning, Cupcake. The Cupcakery features 12 different flavors, plus a cupcake of the month. The simple truth is that you can't stop after just one. Pick up a dozen, or have them delivered. Forget the doughnuts, the cupcakes are here.

9680 S Eastern Avenue, Suite #100, Henderson NV
(702) 207-CAKE (2253)
www.thecupcakery.com

Portraits by Catherine

Catherine, a certified professional photographer, is well known for her portraiture of children, families, graduates and pets. All sessions are by appointment only, giving you time to relax and enjoy your portrait experience. Her Enchanted Children Series puts your child in magical scenes. These scenes range from fairies, angels and mermaids to western, gone fishin' and vintage baseball. Scenes for pets are equally well thought out. The resulting portraits are artistically rendered with precision and skill and are some of the most beautiful you will ever see. You may even see your previews the same day as your session. The studio is completely digital, which means more creativity and fun. The studio is also one of the largest and best equipped in the Las Vegas Valley, accommodating groups of up to twenty-five people. Catherine Guillotte grew up with a photographer father and her work reveals an expert eye and captivating personal style. Visit Portraits by Catherine and bring home a lasting memory. All of her portraits are professionally crafted and personally guaranteed.

2300 N Rainbow Boulevard, #111, Las Vegas NV
(702) 432-3103
www.portraitsbycatherine.com

Ron Lee Gallery

It's not often that you can come into a gallery and meet the artist, but at the Ron Lee Gallery you might just catch a glimpse of him creating his sculptures right on the premises. Ron is the world's leading sculptor of clowns and animation figurines. He begins with clay and finishes in a variety of fine casting materials. Many sculptures are finished with a 24-karat gold finish. All are hand painted and mounted on onyx bases. Ron has been producing clown sculpture in this style since the 1970s. One clown, Hobo Joe, remains Ron's mascot. The thousands of clowns Ron created eventually took his company out of his Canoga Park, California garage and into the gallery scene of the Las Vegas valley. Ron now holds the license with M&M's World. He has produced a new line of limited edition figurines. "I've been creating my whole life. The sales are secondary to the creativity," he says. The gallery also contains Las Vegas-themed sculptures to commemorate your vacation and Warner Brothers animation figurines, such as Bugs Bunny, Yosemite Sam and Daffy Duck. For limited edition sculptures that are playful and humorous, visit the Ron Lee Gallery.

7665 Commercial Way, Suite A, Henderson NV
(702) 434-1700
www.ronlee.com

Mesquite Art & Frame

In its first few years of operation, Mesquite Art & Frame has earned a strong reputation for its selection of local art. The upstairs and downstairs galleries house regularly changing exhibits. Oil paintings and watercolors fill the walls, complemented by freestanding sculptures. Among the 400 pieces on display, you'll always find lithographs, posters and prints that would look good in your home or office. If you are shopping for a gift, Mesquite Art & Frame has jewelry as well as exquisite glass and bronze sculptures. Educational programs include classes, workshops, seminars and lectures. Custom framing is a specialty. No art walk around Mesquite is complete until you have visited this gallery, which is also listed as a historical site. Originally a hotel, the structure features mighty beams across its white stucco ceiling and is more than 100 years old. Proprietors Phil and Brenda Moulton report strange happenings from time to time, leading them to believe that spirits inhabit the place. You'll know you have found Mesquite Art & Frame when you see the bronze sculptures out front. Drop by for an artful experience. You may even encounter one of the resident spirits while contemplating the many art pieces.

220 E Mesquite Boulevard, Mesquite NV (702) 346-6541

Tammy Lier
Mrs. Nevada 2003-2004

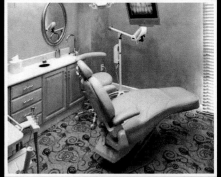

Dr. James Wright

Four Seasons Dental Spa

If you never thought you would look forward to going to the dentist, then you probably haven't tried the luxury services at Four Seasons Dental Spa. In 2003, Dr. James Wright's wife, Debbie, recommended that he make "going to the dentist feel like a visit to a relaxing spa." The result is a Las Vegas dental clinic that is changing attitudes with complementary holistic spa amenities. A concierge will greet you and seat you in a room with plush massage chairs, aromatherapy and a huge saltwater aquarium. Once in the dental chair, you'll receive lip therapy, a warm paraffin hand treatment and jewelry cleaning while you watch your favorite television show. The equipment is state-of-the-art, and your visit is peaceful, thanks to the nearly noiseless drill. After your dental treatment, you can enjoy a full body aquamassage or refresh yourself at the aromatherapy oxygen bar. Your visit closes with a serving of tea, juice or freshly oxygenated water. Patients enjoy lingering at this dental office. For all its amenities, the emphasis remains on exceptional dental care. Beautiful cosmetic veneers are Dr. Wright's passion. He says proudly, "A beautiful new smile is a gift in many ways, because patients are more confident, smile more and look years younger. The cards and letters are so rewarding. We are delighted to hear how a new smile affects someone's life." These extraordinary services attract clients from numerous other states and countries. For services that surpass the Tooth Fairy's wildest dreams, visit Four Seasons Dental Spa.

**8855 W Flamingo Road, Las Vegas NV
(702) 309-4600 or (866) 4-SMILES (764537)**
www.FourSeasonsDentalSpa.com

Ambiance Relaxation Spa

Pam Beckstead has built Ambiance Relaxation Spa on the concepts of personalized service and unhurried treatments. Her desire to help people got her into this business. Having suffered from acne herself, she concentrated on facials when she first opened in 2004. Enthusiastic customers encouraged her to offer other services, such as massage therapy and body treatments. Signature treatments include the yummy Chocolate & Roses. The Soak in the Sea features a therapeutic bath in seawater and seaweed. A salt glow, steam-towel wrap and mineral bath are just the beginning of the Royal Treatment. Limo service is available for this full day of pampering. Couple's packages, another Ambiance specialty, always take place in the same room so that husband and wife don't have to separate. Pam intends to limit the growth of Ambiance to maintain the personal touch. By keeping things small, she can offer outstanding service at affordable prices. What's more, she gets to talk with her clients in depth, which helps her understand their needs. Pam thanks the members of her family who work with her at the spa. Let the personalized difference at Ambiance Relaxation Spa make you feel like the most important person in the world.

2425 W Horizon Ridge Parkway, Henderson NV
(702) 212-2659
www.ambianceofhenderson.com

Healing Hands Chiropractic and Wellness

At Healing Hands Chiropractic and Wellness, Caroline Williams, DC works to align your mind and body as well as your spine. More than a chiropractic office, Healing Hands offers holistic health and wellness consultations and a full range of spa treatments. Dr. Williams' holistic philosophy stipulates that physical, mental and spiritual wellbeing are closely interconnected. "If one area of your life is out of balance, it affects you entirely," she explains. Therefore, Healing Hands offers personalized education in maintaining balance and recommends spa treatments for wellness. Massage is known for its therapeutic and detoxifying benefits. Healing Hands values the European philosophy that healthy skin is beautiful skin and uses Pure Swiss Skin Care products of unparalleled quality for all facials. Healing Hands is also one of the first offices to provide far infrared saunas and educate on the benefits of using one. In contrast to conventional sauna heat, infrared heat penetrates deeply into the body's cells, releasing toxins and heavy metals that may have been stagnant there for years. Infrared saunas can improve circulation, boost the immune system and lower blood pressure. Discover a healthier, happier you through the many resources at Healing Hands Chiropractic and Wellness.

2625 W Horizon Ridge Parkway, Suite 140, Henderson NV
(702) 938-0199
www.healinghandswellness.myarbonne.com

Mesa View Regional Hospital

The days of traveling to St. George or Las Vegas for medical care ended for many Mesquite residents with the opening of Mesa View Regional Hospital in 2004. Part of the Triad hospital system, the 25-bed facility is small but complete with all the necessary radiology equipment, plus well-equipped surgery suites, an emergency trauma room, intensive care unit, and comfortable labor and delivery rooms. The 160 Mesa View staff members are among the kindest caregivers you will find anywhere and more than live up to the hospital's slogan, We Will Care for You. Their services sometimes reach far beyond their job descriptions. People still talk about the staff member who gave a pair of her own shoes to a barefoot woman who was ready for discharge from the emergency room. The compassion at this hospital is equaled by its competence. A national accrediting body found that among Triad's 49 hospitals, Mesa View regularly places among the top in patient satisfaction. Mesquite is a more caring place since the arrival of Mesa View Regional Hospital.

1299 Bertha Howe Avenue, Mesquite NV
(702) 346-8040
www.mesaviewhospital.com

Djanel Spa & Salon

Once an estate, now a lavishly appointed spa and salon, Djanel Spa & Salon specializes in skin care, body care, massage and pampering. Guests come for the experience, not just the services. Let the Djanel limousine pick you up at your hotel and drive you to the front door. Once inside this gorgeous Mediterranean-themed hideaway, you will find eight treatment rooms and a lounge for relaxation and meditation. The spa opens to a courtyard with cabanas and hot tub. There's even a putting green. Slip into a bath filled with rose petals by booking the Goddess Package. A Swedish massage and European facial are part of this full-day of indulgence, which will leave you feeling divine. As with the popular Couples Package, the Goddess Package includes lunch served outdoors in a cabana. Overnight retreats allow clients to rejuvenate completely. They begin with late afternoon spa treatments, followed by a catered dinner. Make your next party an exotic one with belly dancing, fire dancers and live music in the courtyard. The ABC and Fox networks have featured Djanel. It is located just a few minutes from the Strip, though its serene atmosphere seems a world away from the hustle and bustle. Enter Djanel Spa & Salon for relaxation, pampering and replenishment.

5150 S Pecos Road, Las Vegas NV
(702) 868-6000
www.djanelspa.com

Wraptures The Body Wrap Spa

With treatments that leave customers looking six to 20 inches slimmer, you are likely to leave Wraptures The Body Wrap Spa feeling positively rapturous. The Las Vegas spa features The Body Wrap by Suddenly Slender, which has been proven over the course of five decades to result in inch loss by tightening and toning of the skin. The treatment begins by wrapping your body in soft, porous bandages that have been soaked in a solution of food-grade minerals to improve skin health. An hour later, the bandages are removed to reveal the tighter, trimmer you. This treatment has been featured on the *Tyra Banks Show* and in such publications as *Woman's World*. Wraptures Manager Bill Mowery has trained extensively in the application of The Body Wrap, so you're guaranteed a great experience. Wraptures also features the IonCleanse system, which uses energy-charged ions to neutralize tissue acid waste. Many people with swollen or deteriorating joints, gout or edema have reported relief following IonCleanse sessions. You'll also find such dietary supplements as Cellfood, a formula designed to boost energy with oxygen, 78 minerals, 34 enzymes and 17 amino acids. To repair and rejuvenate your skin, try the Cellfood Oxygen Gel. Wraptures also carries products that help with joint care and weight loss. For an experience that will leave you looking and feeling thinner and younger, come to Wraptures The Body Wrap Spa.

4235 S Fort Apache Road, Suite 140, Las Vegas NV
(702) 243-9922
www.wraptureslasvegas.com

The Fertility Center of Las Vegas

Since 1988, the Fertility Center of Las Vegas has given Mother Nature a boost by providing advanced fertility medicine. "There are treatments for virtually every patient," says Medical Director Dr. Bruce Shapiro. Dr. Shapiro and his partner, Dr. Said Daneshmand, are renowned for their innovations in the field of fertility medicine. The Fertility Center offers all fertility services and specializes in greatly reducing the risks of potential complications of in vitro fertilization, including hyperstimulation syndrome and high-order pregnancy. The Fertility Center excels at egg donation and gestational carrier (surrogate) cycles and fertility preservation through embryo and egg freezing. Pre-implantation genetic analysis is available to screen embryos for potential genetic diseases. The nationally accredited center is open daily. Its success rates, knowledgeable staff and comfortable facilities attract clients from around the world, including many fellow MDs. The care and support patients experience here has inspired an annual patient reunion, which has raised over $40,000 for children's charities.

8851 W Sahara Avenue, Suite 100, Las Vegas NV (702) 254-1777 or (800) 509-7174
11251 S Eastern Avenue, Suite 150, Henderson NV (702) 254-1777 or (800) 509-7174
www.FertilityCenterLV.com

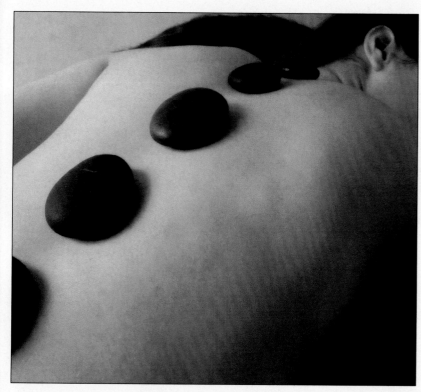

Ki-Atsu Institute for Healing Arts

Whether you come to the Ki-Atsu Institute for Healing Arts as a client or student, Ki Kosut will see to it that you understand the mind, body and spirit connection. Born in France and raised in Australia, Ki is the vessel of positive energy who directs the institute with her husband, Timothy. Ki ran a fitness center in Vanuatu for eight years before coming to America. Collectively Ki and Timothy's titles cover a broad spectrum of expertise, including master hypnotist, NLP practitioner and Reiki master. She's also a yoga and Pilates coach and an Asian Bodywork instructor. People come to the 3,500-square-foot facility to receive treatments and services or to take classes towards certification in one or more of the healing arts. These arts are related in that each is a part of a whole disciplined approach to restructuring, refocusing and restoring your mind, your body and your life. To truly master one is a lifetime pursuit, which is why the Ki-Atsu Institute offers continuing education and private classes beyond its programs for certification. When the staff isn't teaching, it is busy in the therapy rooms, helping clients achieve and maintain balance. The signature treatment is ashiatsu, a realignment technique in which the practitioner applies strokes with his or her bare feet. Make the mind, body and spirit connection at the Ki-Atsu Institute for Healing Arts.

11251 S Eastern Avenue, Suite 180, Henderson NV
(702) 263-9000
www.ki-atsu.com

Applause Salon & Spa

Owner Karen Langford's vision for Applause Salon & Spa is to provide the highest level of customer service in an inviting and relaxed atmosphere. "We are dedicated to the beauty, health and well-being of each and every individual," Langford observes. "At Applause Salon & Spa, you're the star." One look at the salon and spa menus and you'll see that Langford stands by her word. The spa menu features Murad signature facials and body treatments such as the Environmental Shield Vitamin C Infusion Facial and the Firm & Tone Cellulite Body Treatment inspired by the philosophy of Dr. Howard Murad, author of *The Cellulite Solution*. Applause specializes in hair, make-up and nail services as well. Options such as a color, highlights or extensions will help you achieve a new look. Other services include waxing and massage therapy. Hot stone therapy allows deeper muscle penetration during massage and provides a mental lift. The body treatments include a seaweed wrap and a pomegranate body scrub. Anyone experiencing fatigue will be revitalized by hydrotherapy, an aromatherapy bath that takes only 20 minutes. Packages include a six-hour special, the Standing Ovation, which includes a spa lunch. Take the time to improve your life at Applause Salon & Spa.

4180 S Grand Canyon Drive, Las Vegas NV
(702) 228-0123
www.applausesalonspa.com

Milton Homer Fine Home Furnishings

Milton Homer Fine Home Furnishings has been a design leader from the start. Whether you prefer traditional, transitional or contemporary style, Milton Homer has what you need to make your dream home a reality. Twenty thousand square feet of professionally designed room settings showcase fine furnishings and accessories from top-quality manufacturers around the world. Milton Homer's designers are prepared for new and original design work. They offer complete design services and can help with anything from updating a single room to a complete interior design package. The stores' buyers work hard to bring the best products to Las Vegas at affordable prices. Milton Homer Fine Home Furnishings is confident enough about offering the best prices to put its best price guarantee in writing. Milton Homer and his wife, June, started the business in the Bay Area, where Milton's hairstyling clients sought his savvy advice on furnishings and party planning. The Homers later moved to Utah, where they opened a business specializing in home furnishing and interior design. In 1977, they successfully launched Milton Homer Fine Home Furnishings in Las Vegas and later opened another location in the Summerlin area. The family-owned business, now owned by Greg Thomson and daughter Jill Homer Thomson, continues the tradition of bringing fine furniture and good design to the Las Vegas area. For professional design guidance, outstanding customer service and stunning furnishings that express your taste, come to Milton Homer Fine Home Furnishings.

780 S Rampart Boulevard, Las Vegas NV
(702) 948-0707
5455 S Valley View Boulevard, Las Vegas NV
(702) 798-0707
www.miltonhomer.com

Furniture Market

At Furniture Market, Liz and Robert Werner want their customers to be completely happy with their experience. That's why the couple insist on doing nearly everything themselves—from filling their store with stylish furniture to providing top-notch customer service from behind the counter. Of course, they do accept some help from their hardworking daughters, Devon and Ryan, who display an equally dedicated work ethic. Scary price tags won't daunt the patrons here. The Werners scour the World Market Center for the best deals and order directly from manufacturers to pass those savings along to their customers. The result is a showroom stocked with the latest styles in home furnishings at a price you can afford. This family-run business has been bringing affordable and beautiful furniture to Las Vegas-area residents since 2005. Browse through the aisles of classic and contemporary furnishings at Furniture Market and you'll be sure to find something to suit your style and your budget.

6675 S Eastern Avenue, Las Vegas NV
(702) 436-3960

Vizion

If you appreciate streamlined design combined with function and classic comfort, Vizion carries the styles you seek. Owners Paul and Christie Mikkelsen showcase a clean-lined mix of contemporary and Scandinavian furniture in their upscale store. Paul, originally from Denmark, had worked in the furniture business in Houston for more than a decade before opening the store. The couple envisioned Las Vegas, the fastest-growing city in the United States, as the perfect place for their store and opened Vizion in 2002. Vizion features the Stressless system by Ekornes, a registered brand of Scandinavian leather furniture that features a patented ergonomic design that supports you perfectly, whether upright or reclining. Each sofa seat adjusts individually as well, and recliners come in two or three sizes to fit all body types and sizes. Expect to find functional furniture for your home theater, office, bedroom, living room and dining room, as well as thoughtfully chosen accessories. Vizion also offers reproductions of classic contemporary seating pieces designed originally by Mies Van Der Rohe, Marcel Breuer and Le Corbusier. You can special order furniture in your chosen color and finish. An interior design service helps you plan a space to suit your personality and style. For sleek furnishings, well-spaced displays and knowledgeable staff, come browse at the Vizion showroom.

5240 S Decatur Boulevard, Suite 5, Las Vegas NV
(702) 365-5240
www.vizionfurniture.com

Northern Lights

Northern Lights has been illuminating Las Vegas since 1997, when owners Eric Peterson and Troy Simmons teamed up to create this residential lighting and home accessory mecca. A family-owned business right from the start, Northern Lights originated as a 1,400-square-foot lighting store. They quickly outgrew that space, and now offer two locations, each with a showroom of more than 4,000 square feet filled with fixtures, table lamps, floor lamps, ceiling fans and more. With merchandise to accommodate any budget, their prices range from less than $50 to more than $10,000. Lighting is just a fraction of what you'll find at Northern Lights. They feature many unique home items to stimulate your senses, such as decorative sinks, wall hangings, artwork and mirrors. Feast your eyes on unique vases, planters, candleholders and wall clocks. Drive on over to the northwest or southeast corners of the valley. It's where you will find Troy or Eric hanging out with their dogs, ready to offer you a touch of Northern Lights.

5060 S Fort Apache Road, Las Vegas NV (Summerlin) (702) 396-6963
9302 S Eastern Avenue, Las Vegas NV (Green Valley) (702) 270-4145
6125 S Valley View, Las Vegas NV (Central)   (702) 438-6600
www.northernlightslv.com

Crowne Closets & Cabinetry

Crowne Closets & Cabinetry offers attractive storage solutions for every room in your home. "We custom design a storage and organizational solution for our customers," says Steven R. Mann, President of Crowne Closets & Cabinetry. Storage can make or break a living space, and Crowne's storage options are customized to fit your rooms and your stuff. Whether you're looking to store books in library shelves or hide a bed in a wall, Crowne consultants can determine your needs and present a computerized overview of your project. "We have clients who literally have our cabinetry in every room of their home," says Steven. Crowne offers custom-designed entertainment centers built to the exact specifications of your living room, as well as cabinetry for home offices, closets, pantries and laundry rooms. Your garage will feel spacious once again when your tools and toys fit snuggly behind closed doors. You can reclaim that spare bedroom with stylish built-ins that keep the bed off the floor when it's not needed. In 1993, Crowne had eight employees, two installation crews and a 3,000-square-foot factory. Today, it boasts 180-plus employees, 23 installation crews and a 38,000-square-foot factory. "We maintained quality, increased our product line and stressed customer service," says Steven. Reclaim your floor space, organize your possessions and beautify your home with storage solutions from Crowne Closets & Cabinetry.

5030 W Oquendo Road, Las Vegas NV
(702) 739-0000
www.crowneclosets.com

Water Creations

Ken Caouette knows a lot about making a splash in your backyard. He built pools and spas in Southern California before opening Water Creations with his wife, Denice, in Las Vegas in 1997. "We've never designed the same pool; it's always new and different," Kenneth says. Each pool is initially created on a computer that lets buyers take a virtual tour of their recreated backyard. Water Creations focuses on making sure the pool and yard are part of what Ken calls "the complete outdoor package." He goes on to say, "It's not just about digging a hole in the ground and putting water in it. We design the yard and take the architecture of the home into consideration." Options range from futuristic designs, such as the infinity edge pool, which gives the illusion of water suspended in midair, to man-made rock with grottos, caves and slides. Water Creations' high level of customer service and craftsmanship caused the editors of *Las Vegas Life* magazine to name the company as the area's Best Pool Builder. If you're looking for a pool that suits your home and yard, it's time you visited the experts at Water Creations.

3800 E Patrick Lane, Suite #3, Las Vegas NV
(702) 739-3093
www.watercreationslv.com

Colleen's Classic Consignment

Since 1995, Colleen Aiken has been the person to see when you want to buy or sell quality used and new furniture in Las Vegas. "I get chills from the eclectic pieces that our customers get from our stores and the great pricing," says Colleen, owner of Colleen's Classic Consignment. Her two stores feature new and gently used furniture in all styles with prices that beat retail store pricing by 50 to 80 percent. Whether it's a sofa, table or easy chair you seek, you'll find the major brands here as well as unusual items to beautify and personalize your home. New pieces arrive daily, assuring the showroom remains fresh and deserving of your frequent visits. If you've got furniture to sell, Colleen's can help. Most consigned furniture sells within the first month, with many pieces sold the first day they appear in the showroom. By selling furnishings through Colleen's, you avoid the hassle of pricing, advertising and opening your home to strangers. Colleen's will even come to your house and pick up your furniture item. Once it sells, you'll receive a check. Whether you're buying or selling, you'll appreciate the friendly, knowledgeable staff who assures that every phase of your experience will be satisfactory. To buy or sell attractive furniture, come to Colleen's Classic Consignment.

3071 N Rainbow Boulevard, Suite 100, Las Vegas NV (702) 247-7602
7380 S Eastern Avenue, Las Vegas NV (702) 951-7008
www.colleensclassicconsignment.com

Sunset Spas

Sunset Spas in Henderson offers a variety of high quality spas, spa accessories and garden gazebos at reasonable prices. The new owner, who has extensive experience in the spa industry, cares about his product and the people buying it, which means you can expect some superior customer service along with superior selection, products and pricing. He calls on years of experience to help educate customers about spas so that they can make informed buying decisions. Sunset Spas carries top-of-the-line Dynasty spas crafted from synthetic materials for strength and longevity. The store showcases at least 15 different models; higher end models come equipped with everything from stereos to mood lighting. Expect to find a wide range of spa accessories as well, including stairs, scents and side tables. Consider adding the soothing sounds of a waterfall or the nighttime drama of fiber optic lighting to your spa setup. A misting system can provide cooling comfort on warm days. Service at Sunset Spas is personalized, and staff members do their best to find any spa part that you need, even if it's not a brand that they carry. They will be happy to special order parts they don't have in stock. You'll find four different types of gazebos at Sunset Spas, which will add beauty and privacy to your spa setup. When you're ready for a spa and gazebo, come check out the service and selection at Sunset Spas.

520 Marks Street, Suite 130, Henderson NV
(702) 451-2228

Futon Lifestyle Furniture

A futon mattress, cover and frame provide a couch and bed in one affordable piece of furniture. For that reason, college kids without a lot of money have long favored them. If you have always thought of futons as practical but not very stylish, then a visit to Futon Lifestyle Furniture will quickly change your mind. Beautiful hardwood frames elegant enough for your living room share showroom space with basic pieces suitable for a guest room. In all, owner Tony Sciame stocks as many as 50 different varieties of futons at any given time. Certain classic looks are mainstays, while new models appear every couple of months. Futon Lifestyle Furniture also carries platform beds, couches and loveseats. "I want people to have as much information about futons as possible," says Tony, who enjoys helping customers find the perfect harmony of frame, mattress and cover to fit their needs. In a comparison with sofa beds, futons win every time, he notes. Their mattresses are thicker, their look is more appealing, they usually cost less and they are generally easier to fold out and up. Drop by Futon Lifestyle Furniture and be amazed at how far futons have come.

2555 E Tropicana Avenue, Las Vegas NV
(702) 451-4488

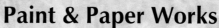

Paint & Paper Works

Paint & Paper Works is the place to visit if you want to go far beyond merely painting your walls. It is the largest and most comprehensive faux finishing company in the Las Vegas area. Paint & Paper Works has been in business for 23 years and in Las Vegas for seven years. You are invited to browse the 3,000-square-foot showroom. Using decorative painting and faux finishes, the professionals at Paint & Paper Works can transform your living space into your own special surroundings, creating drama or fun for everyone to enjoy. Faux painting adds color, dimension and depth, encouraging your eyes to travel around the room. At Paint & Paper Works creativity is limitless. The custom-blended glazes create unusual colorwashes and enhance the eye-catching plaster finishes. The textural products and innovative ideas combine into techniques that enable the staff to reproduce natural finishes, such as woods, marble, metals, stone and fabrics, with tremendous realism and durability. Paint & Paper Works can create aged-crackle, rusted metals, patinas, frescoes, gold leaf, metallic and pearl finishes. The staff can also create geometric designs and stripes, whimsical sky's, ragged and sponged techniques and hand-painted or stenciled designs. The varied selections of finishes are customized for each client. Paint & Paper Works prides itself in being the best, using personally trained artisans. With a reputation based on one-of-a-kind custom finishes, quality workmanship and excellent customer services, Paint & Paper Works is the place to go. Visitors can even take advantage of a free home-consultation.

4310 S Cameron Street, Suite 1, Las Vegas NV
(702) 362-8306
www.paintpaperworks.com
www.virtualtoursvegas.com

Plant World Nursery

Visitors to Plant World Nursery experience a little bit of the desert, the tropics and several climates in between. Plant World's huge greenhouse is full of indoor and outdoor flowering species. Among the 1,000 different plant varieties in stock, you will find cacti, which do well in arid Nevada, along with plants that thrive almost anywhere. Vegetable gardeners come to Plant World Nursery for its many varieties of tomatoes, peppers and herbs. The menagerie of store pets makes the shopping experience special. If the macaws and toucans are sounding off as you enter the store, you'll think you've walked into a tropical rain forest. Be sure to check out the giant African tortoise, too. If you are shopping for garden tools and supplies, you won't be disappointed. There's an impressive selection, and Nelson the cat just might follow you down the aisle to see what you're doing. Plant World Nursery, a Las Vegas fixture since 1967, is also the place to find pottery planters, bird feeders and wind chimes. Complete landscape installation is a specialty, as is landscape maintenance. For vast selection and a delightful shopping experience, head for Plant World Nursery.

5301 W Charleston Boulevard, Las Vegas NV
(702) 878-9485 *www.plantworldnursery.com*

Seton Academy Private Preschool & Kindergarten

Seton Academy was established to meet the needs of children in the Las Vegas area. Psychologists and educators agree that more learning takes place during the first five years of a child's life than at any other period. It is with this in mind that Seton Academy has planned its school program and prepared an environment which will aid the development of the young child—socially, physically, emotionally and intellectually. The original Seton Academy, founded in 1963 by Tony and Mary Drago, was the first unaffiliated preschool in Las Vegas. Tony died in 1978 and Mary later married Matthew Hayes. A well-respected educator of young children, Mrs. Hayes has a bachelor degree in education and is a long-time member of the National Association for the Education of Young Children. Mrs. Hayes oversees the programs at both campuses as the Executive Director. Her family is also involved in many facets of the business. Through her dedication and skill, over 8,500 children have benefited from the Seton learning experience and, now into its second generation, Seton Academy Preschool and Kindergarten continues to be one of Las Vegas' finest. Seton Academy offers its students academic instruction, living skills and fun, according to a time-tested program created and perfected by Mrs. Hayes and her experienced staff. The academy is extremely fortunate to maintain a long-standing staff of expert teachers. Seton Academy is the longest licensed preschool in Clark County, Las Vegas. It was named the Best in the City by *Las Vegas Magazine* in December 2001 and the Premier Preschool and Kindergarten in Las Vegas.

3801 N Campbell Road, Las Vegas NV
(702) 233-2069
9975 Placid Street, Las Vegas NV
(702) 736-4246
www.setonacademypreschool.com

Las Vegas Day School

Jack and Helen Daseler were pioneers in the field of education who envisioned a non-sectarian, non-denominational private school where students could discover their full potential. Their school, the Las Vegas Day School, was the first of its kind in the state of Nevada. It began in 1961 as a one-room schoolhouse with just 27 students. Currently it has an enrollment of approximately 825 students in preschool through eighth grade. Taking pride in one's work and developing good study habits are emphasized from the start in a rigorous academic program centered on the three R's. The school offers not only a curriculum that stimulates children but a disciplined and safe environment where they can grow and develop socially as well as emotionally. The highly qualified and compassionate teachers embrace the joy of learning on a daily basis. The pupil to teacher ratio varies by grade level with an average of 20 to one. The single biggest reason that parents send their children to Las Vegas Day School, says Director Neil H. Daseler, is to give them every advantage that a quality education can provide for high school, college and their adult business life. The mission of the school is to foster each individual student to grow and develop as a self-assured, dedicated learner who will shape the future of our society. Consider a campus tour to learn more about Las Vegas Day School.

3275 Red Rock Street, Las Vegas NV
(702) 362-1180
www.LVDS.com

The Art Institute of Las Vegas

With a curriculum that stretches from 3-D computer animation to culinary arts, The Art Institute of Las Vegas and The Culinary Institute of Las Vegas (a division of The Art Institute) provide students with the skills they need to become creative professionals. The school has served the Las Vegas area since 1983, becoming part of the nationwide family of Art Institutes in 2001. The institute specializes in design, media arts and culinary arts, offering both associate's and bachelor's degrees. Technologically minded students with an interest in media can earn degrees in such fields as digital media production or game art & design. A degree in interior design prepares the recipient to design both residential and commercial spaces. Still another avenue of creative pursuit here is the culinary arts program, which can get you started with entry-level positions in the food industry or prepare you for culinary management with a Bachelor of Science degree. Education at The Art Institute of Las Vegas is hands-on, with opportunities to gain valuable experience in the field prior to graduating. Students can also take advantage of career services, including job fairs and advisors who help students take advantage of employment opportunities. The school provides a nurturing environment, where creative students thrive. Financial aid is available. If you dream of a career in design, media arts or culinary arts, investigate the possibilities at The Art Institute of Las Vegas.

2350 Corporate Circle, Henderson NV
(702) 369-9944 or (800) 833-2678
www.artinstitutes.edu/lasvegas

Cottages of Green Valley

The Cottages of Green Valley in Henderson provide a balance between the need for assistance and the desire for independence. They feature single-story cottages grouped around a central courtyard and community center. Each cottage serves 12 residents who share a living room, family room and dining room. Each resident has their own spacious suite within the cottage, which includes a private bath and plenty of room for furniture. The home-like setting has the feel of a neighborhood and allows residents to build relationships and stay connected to other residents. The Cottages of Green Valley feature family-style dining in each cottage so that residents can eat together in their own dining room. They also utilize two activity directors, one for assisted living and one for memory care. Many activities take place in Rose Hall and Pine Lodge, the community centers, including bingo, movies, arts and crafts, exercise and entertainment. Around the clock staffing and a high ratio of caregivers to residents ensure excellent care. Memory care cottages feature specially trained caregivers who work with families and professionals to provide compassionate care for residents with memory problems. Respite care is available. Experience the best of both worlds—independent living and assistance as needed—when you come home to the Cottages of Green Valley.

2620 Robindale Road, Henderson NV (702) 992-0000 *www.cottagesgv.com*

Las Vegas Mini Gran Prix

Las Vegas Mini Gran Prix puts the whole family on wheels. "Everybody, no matter how old they are, can have fun here," says owner Jerry Barton. Since 1992, this entertainment center has offered rides and activities designed for kids and adults to do together, including many rides you won't find anywhere else in the state. The business offers four tracks for varied thrills. It's wheel-to-wheel action on the Sprint Kart Speedway and a good time for children as young as four on the Kiddie Karts track. Kids, with or without an adult, can test their skills on the longest go-kart track in Nevada. You'll also find an adult track with vehicles that require a valid driver's license. Beyond the tracks, look for such amusement rides as the Dive Bomber and the Tornado Twister. An expanded arcade offers favorite games, including a few that might be new to you. No doubt you'll be ready for a meal or snack after all this activity. Pizza, sandwiches, chicken wings and tenders, even fresh-baked cookies, are waiting in the restaurant. Jerry has been in the family amusement business since the 1970s and personally laid out the park's design. He adds new attractions each year and invites you to visit the park for a corporate event, church gathering or kid's birthday party. The park has won the Governor's Tourism Award and been listed as a top 100 attraction in *LV Life* magazine. For safe family fun, come to Las Vegas Mini Gran Prix.

1401 N Rainbow Boulevard, Las Vegas NV
(702) 259-7000 or (800) 259-RACE (7223)
www.lvmgp.com

FitnessBeast

With FitnessBeast on your side, you can go on a rampage against extra pounds and flab. FitnessBeast sells treadmills, weights, home gyms and many other types of exercise equipment. President and CEO Anthony Zaino opened the Henderson store in 2005 after managing a similar store in Chicago. FitnessBeast features all the top brands representing the best quality fitness equipment in the business. From cardio queen to bodybuilder, FitnessBeast has the right equipment. "Our customers can get knowledgeable and personalized training and information on the product," Anthony says. The friendly staff can help you pick the right pieces of fitness equipment for your goals and then follow up with exercise and nutritional advice to make sure you really reach your goal. The store offers free in-home delivery and setup of any equipment, and FitnessBeast also sells online throughout the United States.

6250 Mountain Vista, Henderson NV
(702) 368-2005 or (800) 437-0560
www.fitnessbeast.com

The Laughlin Bay Marina

Boat owners who store their vessels at the Laughlin Bay Marina enjoy valet launch service—by calling ahead, they find their boat fueled up and on the water upon their arrival. It's just part of the exceptional service that the staff of 40 has proudly provided since the grand opening in 2005. Nestled in a protected lagoon four miles downstream from the Laughlin casino area, the Laughlin Bay Marina provides a convenient turn-around point for boats on the Colorado River. The marina sports a luxury clubhouse, a five-story storage structure for 150 boats and about 110 slips to accommodate boats of various sizes. The marina is noteworthy for its good looks. Its white buildings gleam in contrast to the blue waters of the lagoon. Some of the nicest white-sand beaches in the area accumulate on the shores of the marina to the western end of the lagoon. The reed stands and open water areas beyond the main navigation channel are open only to non-powered craft. Plentiful wildlife make this area ideal for fishing and bird watching. The marina project is a vision of renowned architect Samuel Wacht. The lighthouse tower feature is the centerpiece of the marina administration building, which houses the Bistro, a full service restaurant and bar. The clubhouse provides peaceful views of the lagoon and has hosted many special events. The marina is part of an envisioned community of 500 condominiums called The Landing. In a few years, when the river walk is completed, you'll be able to walk straight into the city of Laughlin from the marina. Make the Laughlin Bay Marina part of your Colorado River experience.

4040 Marina Lagoon Drive, Laughlin NV
(702) 298-0775
www.laughlinbaymarina.com

Soaring Center

Passengers really do feel the wind beneath their wings during a glider ride at the Soaring Center. Located in Jean, the Soaring Center is owned by Michael and Karen Henderson, who have more than 30 years of experience sailing the skies. Michael and Karen previously owned a similar business in Washington, but moved to Nevada, where the more temperate weather allows them to fly year-round. Soaring Center is the only commercial soaring school and glider ride business in southern Nevada. You'll thrill to the experience as a glider carries you aloft on the currents while it provides an eagle's eye view of the awe-inspiring desert. Looking for a thrill ride? Try one of the aerobatic rides. Though each ride is thrilling, the Soaring Center takes every precaution to guarantee your safety. The Center offers group activities for parties of up to 30 people. Two large barbecues and other amenities keep the folks on the ground busy. Want to learn to fly a glider on your own? The Soaring Center offers professional training for both pilots and non-pilots, in addition to equipment rentals. Glide on in to the Soaring Center for a fantastic flight.

23600 S Las Vegas Boulevard, Jean NV
(702) 874-1010
www.soaringcenter.net

American Cactus Divers

Imagine entering a tranquil world where sound escapes you while your other senses come to life, and your body shivers delightfully as underwater figures slide past your weightless, hovering form. If this sounds like your kind of adventure, then check out American Cactus Divers, where Jerry Yost and the Yost family can train you to become a top-rate diver. Jerry was originally a flight instructor in search of a new challenge when he happened upon diving and thought it sounded like great fun. Turns out he was right, and by 1991, he had fully embraced the diving lifestyle and opened American Cactus Divers, listed as a five-Star facility by the Professional Association of Diving Instruction. Jerry and his team make many diving trips to Lake Mead and offer hands-on diving instruction with an emphasis on safety. Students practice dives in a pool as well as in open water. In addition to offering top-rate dive instruction, American Cactus Divers also offers a selection of underwater scooters and other dive equipment. Jerry serves as president of the Scuba Retailers Association for Nevada, so you're always guaranteed to receive the best products available and sound advice on maintenance, care and safety of your diving equipment. Plot your escape to an underwater world of new colors, shapes and sensations with American Cactus Divers.

3985 E Sunset Road, Las Vegas NV
(702) 433-DIVE (3483)
www.americancactusdivers.com

Master Seong's Black Belt World

Master Seong's Black Belt World in Las Vegas offers comprehensive tae kwon do training for children, teens and adults of every skill level. Translated loosely, the term tae kwon do means *the way of the foot and hand*. This Korean martial art form is based on a constant striving for excellence with the aim of becoming an honorable person with good character and physical condition. Tae kwon do offers a full-contact, cardio workout which develops strength, speed, balance, flexibility and stamina. Students learn self-defense through punches, jabs, chops, blocking moves and powerful leaping kicks. Tae kwon do also imparts discipline and builds such qualities as self-control, respect and self-confidence. The physical and mental benefits of tae kwon do are achievable regardless of the student's age, making tae kwon do an excellent choice for the entire family. Master Jo Seong, a 6th dan with 17 years teaching experience, is an international champion with black belts in tae kwon do and hapkido. In 2002, Master Seong was honored with the Presidential Sports award, and in 1998, he was an airborne division instructor for the Korean Special Forces. Master Seong's teaching strengths include discipline, high energy, passion and the development of strong positive rapport with his students. Black Belt World's students attend class two to six times a week. Students progress through the tae kwon do curriculum at their own rate, earning and testing for a higher ranking, which is signified by a belt of a particular color. Master Seong keeps these belts and other tae kwon do gear in stock. Whether you want to enjoy the many benefits of tae kwon do for yourself or watch your children as they progress to their full potential, count on Master Seong's Black Belt World for world-class instruction.

3945 S Durango Drive, Suite A-10, Las Vegas NV (702) 364-0300 *www.blackbeltworldnevada.com*

Ariginal Fitness

Jason Lutz of Ariginal Fitness in Henderson creates a personalized program for each of his clients that provides the proper combination of nutrition, strength and flexibility training, cardiovascular training and positive attitude to enable them to achieve their fitness goals. A Certified Strength and Conditioning Specialist with a bachelor's degree in exercise physiology from Central Michigan University, Jason looks carefully at each person's challenges and takes into account how lifestyle and work conditions can affect physical health. As an independent fitness coach, Jason works with clients either in their homes or in fitness centers. He holds his clients accountable for sticking to a healthy diet and exercise plan. He advises clients that the best time of day to work out is first thing in the morning, before work or family issues interfere, and that consistent exercise of the proper intensity is the key to getting results. "I want to empower them where they can be truly fit for the long term, not just a reunion or wedding," says Jason. He explains that the word *diet* has a temporary connotation to it and that making any temporary change to your lifestyle will only have temporary results. For a trainer who is committed to delivering results using a truly comprehensive and personalized approach, call Jason at Ariginal Fitness and get started on the new, improved version of you.

6977 Graceful Cloud Avenue, Henderson NV
(702) 525-1010
www.ariginalfitness.com

The Bike Shop

What do you like to feel beneath your wheels when you are biking? Whether the answer is smooth pavement or rugged mountain terrain, the Bike Shop has the bike for you. "We're here to meet your cycling needs," says owner Terry Pittman, who was once a competitive biker. Now he spends his days helping other racers go for the gold. Equipping families with safe, comfortable bikes brings him joy as well. A part of the neighborhood since 1999, the Biking Shop carries a large selection of recreational bikes, hybrids, racing cycles, BMX and mountain bikes to serve everyone from the leisure rider to the daredevil. It is the only dealer of Trek bikes in Henderson. You will always find top-quality biking apparel in stock, including shorts, tops and shoes. Other merchandise includes repair tools and nutritional food items. The friendly, knowledgeable folks who work for Terry at the Bike Shop are all passionate bicyclists. When you come in to buy a bike or have your bike repaired, you'll meet people who love their jobs. If you are new to the area, the staff can tell you about the best trails and routes for your favorite type of biking. Find what you need for your next two-wheeled adventure at the Bike Shop.

2578 Wigwam Parkway, Henderson NV
(702) 897-1618
www.bikeshoplv.com

Silver State Old West Horse Tours

Cowboy up with Silver State Old West Horse Tours and get ready for the ride of your life. Silver State offers good old-fashioned horseback riding tours to Red Rock Canyon. From sun up to sun down, they start their tours from the Spring Mountain Ranch in the Red Rock Canyon Conservation Area. A shuttle picks you up from your hotel and takes you to the ranch located about 30 minutes from the strip. Wranglers greet you, familiarize you with the territory, and show you some horsemanship fundamentals. The horses are great here, so you don't have to worry about being an experienced rider. The trail ride takes you along the historic Old Spanish National Historic Trail. Established along a loose network of Indian footpaths crossing the Colorado Plateau and the Mojave Desert, The Old Spanish Trail was known as the shortest path to riches between Los Angeles and Santa Fe. Silver State offers a Sun-Up horseback ride and a Cowboy Sunset dinner ride. Whichever you choose, you will find yourself immersed in the natural wonders of the Red Rock Canyon, where wild horses, burrows and bighorn still frolic. The ride ends at the Old West Village, which sports an indoor dining pavilion and outdoor eating area where you can grab a light lunch or a steak for dinner. The Village features an old fashioned mercantile, first aid center, jail and livery stable. You can watch a gunfight, or a whip and roping demonstration. Silver State has recently partnered with Awesome Adventures, which offers a wide range of adventure outings, including ATV and mountain bike tours, kayak tours of Lake Mead and more. The next time you're in Las Vegas, visit Silver State Old West Horse Tours, and don't forget your camera. This is an experience you'll want to share with the friends back home.

11652 Royal Derwent Drive, Las Vegas NV
(800) 519-2243
www.adventureseekers.info

Fern Adair
Conservatory of the Arts

For more than 30 years, the Fern Adair Conservatory of the Arts has been teaching toes to tap and making feet fleet. Fern Adair Criddle, the conservatory's owner, formerly owned several dance studios in California. She fell in love with Las Vegas and opened a facility in 1974 with her husband, Ray. That early space was just 800 square feet in size. Now, with more than 21,000 square feet, the conservatory serves as a practice area for some of the biggest performers in Las Vegas and the world, including Celine Dion and Lord of the Dance Michael Flatley. The conservatory offers performance classes for every age and skill level. You'll find classes in ballet, jazz or newer styles such as hip-hop. Instructors include professional dancers who have worked in Broadway musicals, in MTV productions and at Radio City Music Hall. The conservatory also offers coursework in gymnastics and tumbling, as well as piano and vocal lessons. Students are heavily involved in the community and put on many performances and events for the enjoyment of local residents. Concert Fantast and Fantasy are major production concerts generating donations to local children's charities. Come to Fern Adair Conservatory of the Arts for lessons that can set the stage for a career in the performing arts.

3265 E Patrick Lane, Las Vegas NV
(702) 458-7575
www.fernadair.com

Photo © Rio Secco Golf

Rio Secco Golf Club

Take in panoramic views of Las Vegas Valley and the Black Mountains while savoring an 18-hole championship golf course at Rio Secco Golf Club. This full-service golf club, owned and operated by Rio All-Suites Hotel and Harrah's Entertainment, was completed in 1997 and serves both hotel guests and the public. Rees Jones, one of the world's top golf architects, designed the 7,322-yard, par-72 course, which *Golf Digest* rates as one of America's 100 Greatest Public Golf Courses. The Las Vegas PGA membership poll also gives this course a number one ranking among Nevada's public access courses. Four teeing grounds make the course enjoyable for every skill level. Rio Secco features a stunning 30,000-square-foot European-style clubhouse, home to Janelas Restaurant, a large pro shop and a clubroom for VIP guests. The pros at the Butch Harmon School of Golf can teach you to golf or help you shave a few points from your game. In 2002, *Golf Digest* named Butch Harmon Best Golf Instructor in the World. This popular course also offers a unique T-mate program that allows you to reserve the services of a physically fit young woman to act as your golf concierge and hostess. Your T-Mate will greet you upon arrival, maintain your scorecard, move carts, get supplies and ensure that your day at Rio Secco is ideal. Experience golf at its finest with a day at the Rio Secco Golf Club.

2851 Grand Hills Henderson NV
(888) 867-3226
www.riosecco.net

A Wind of Change Kites

The kites at A Wind of Change Kites are a bit beyond what you'll find at a toy store. Since 2001, A Wind of Change has dealt in professional kites that can handle loads of stress, and it specializes in the sport of power kiting. Power kites can be small and fun for recreational flying or they can be as large as small cars. They are designed for considerable power and pull and can be flown with non-motorized vehicles such as kite buggies, roller blades or off-road skateboards. Owner Kent Kingston considers both kite buggying and kite snowboarding to be serious sports and loves to share his passion and knowledge with enthusiasts all over the world. Kent provides kiting education to his customers, in large part because kiting has become so innovative over the last few years. New designs, new materials and improved technology make kites of today more advanced and easier to fly than ever before. You don't have to run to get a kite aloft nowadays and tails are only for decoration. With the advent of high-tech kites and space-age materials, you only need a little bit of wind or no wind at all. New, super ultra-lite kites can even be flown indoors. At A Wind of Change, you'll find high quality, professionally designed kites suitable for all skill levels, wind conditions and purposes. A Wind of Change Kites has the largest inventory of kites in Nevada and also carries giant single-line kites for kite display events, in sizes up to 10,000 square feet. Kent grew up in Salt Lake City in a family that loved kiting, and he now shares that activity with his own kids. Stop by the shop soon and let Kent introduce you to the high-flying world at A Wind of Change Kites.

3870 W Russell Road, Las Vegas NV (702) 736-1476
www.awindofchange.com

Las Vegas Indoor Soccer

If you're looking for sports-oriented recreation away from the scorching heat of a southern Nevada summer, step into Las Vegas Indoor Soccer, where kids and adults can participate in league or recreational play. This huge venue offers soccer instruction to children as young as 18 months. It also features summer camps from June to late August that teach basketball, soccer, dodge ball and flag football. Owner Meir Cohen offers a motivational place for kids of all skill levels to play and learn. All Sports Camp is 11 weeks of non-stop action in everything from flag football to karate, while the Knights Academy aims the action at soccer training and practicing with the Las Vegas Knights. Mighty Mini Morning Camp gives youngsters three to five a morning of crafts, stories and games. Mad Science Camp will bring out the curiosity in a child, while Princess Camp combines sports with such activities as fixing hair and nails and making jewelry. Leagues are divided by age groups and skill levels. Newcomers can check out the facility at the regularly scheduled free open house sessions. Adults can get in on the action by joining one of many women's, men's or co-ed indoor leagues. Parents can also get a great workout during their child's classes in the Studio, which offers dance fitness classes. Beat the heat at Las Vegas Indoor Soccer.

1400 N Rampart Boulevard, Las Vegas NV
(702) 233-3600
www.lasvegasindoorsoccer.com

DragonRidge Country Club

DragonRidge Country Club is the answer to that age-old question, how does one build a golf course in the desert? Located within the MacDonald Highlands luxury community in Henderson, Nevada, DragonRidge is the creation of visionary Rich MacDonald, who wanted an 18-hole championship golf course that would be both challenging and fun. The terrain in the area is unique. DragonRidge was sculpted out of the McCullough Mountains, so it was vital to work with the integrity of the land. Rich hired award-winning architect Jay Moorish and notable architect David Druzisky to design the DragonRidge course and their collaboration really paid dividends. DragonRidge is a five-star course with breathtaking views and non-stop elevation changes. Tiger Woods has played at DragonRidge several times and refers to the course with just one word—incredible. The par-72 course covers 7,032 yards. Strategically placed bunkers, preserved natural rock outcroppings and desert washes will challenge your shot selection. The fairways are generous, allowing golfers of all handicaps to make playable shots from the tee. The greens are phenomenal and the material used under the turf is the best available. Tiger Woods enjoys DragonRidge so much that the Country Club has hosted Tiger Jam III and IV in recent years. Land that was once thought to be too hilly and rocky to develop is now a masterpiece. DragonRidge Country Club is a fully private facility with membership opportunities available.

552 S Stephanie Street, Henderson NV
(702) 614-4444
www.dragonridgecountryclub.com

Photos © Cascata Golf Club

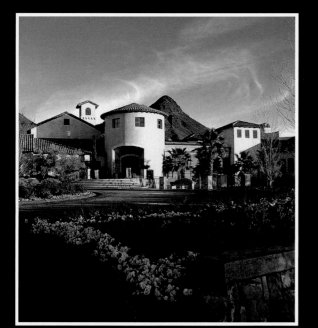

Cascata Golf Club

Cascata Golf Club offers a challenging and enjoyable course designed by the renowned golf course architect Rees Jones. The club was named Cascata, the Italian word for *waterfall*, because of the glorious 418-foot waterfall that flows from the steep mountainside, tumbles over mammoth boulders and cascades into a river that then roars through the clubhouse to eventually settle into a tranquil stream. This perfect blending of the area's natural beauty with the many functions of the 37,000-square-foot Tuscan-style clubhouse is just one of the attributes that caused *Sports Illustrated* to call Cascata "golf's hidden treasure." The clubhouse offers a relaxing venue for dining on gourmet cuisine, enjoying a cigar in the well-stocked cigar lounge or shopping for equipment, clothing or golf accessories at the golf shop. Holes on the 18-hole course are visually isolated from one another and designed for all skill levels. Experienced caddies accompany players on every round and multiple tee locations at each hole allow for varied ranges of play. The lush surroundings attract abundant wildlife, and you are likely to see bighorn sheep, birds and other animals sipping from the streams in the early morning. Savor a day of luxurious service, fine cuisine, natural beauty and, of course, a great game of golf at Cascata Golf Club, just 30 minutes from the Las Vegas Strip.

1 Cascata Drive, Boulder City NV
(702) 294-2000 or (877) 727-4427
www.cascatagolf.com

Skydive Las Vegas

Skydive Las Vegas has been jumping out of Boulder City since 1993. A member of the United States Parachute Association, it is the first and oldest USPA skydiving school in Nevada. Skydive Las Vegas specializes in first-time skydivers. They literally jump with hundreds of first-timers each month. They understand it's not everyday you jump out of a plane. Manager Brent Buckner and his experienced team remember how they felt the first time they jumped. When you take your first jump, you'll be teamed up with a tandem master, who is your personal one-on-one coach. He's there to walk and talk you through every step of the way. If you want, he'll do everything for you. Your harness, the parachute and the tandem master's harness are all connected together with bolts that are rated to hold 10,000 pounds. You may be jumping out of a plane, but there is no question you're in this together. The parachutes are double in size to hold two people. The larger chute also makes for softer openings and landings. After an hour of on-the-ground training, practicing, and gearing up, a Cessna takes you and your tandem master up to 7,000 or 15,000 feet, it's up to you. How long do you want to free-fall? The free fall from 15,000 feet lasts about 50-60 seconds. At almost three miles above sea level you can see the Las Vegas Strip, Hoover Dam, Lake Mead, the Colorado River, Valley of Fire, Mt. Charleston, Redrock Canyon, and four States. The ripcord is pulled at about 4,500 feet for five to seven minutes of quiet, peaceful, soaring and gliding. For an eagle's perspective and a thrill unlike any other, call Skydive Las Vegas and book one of these amazing dives.

1401 Airport Road, Boulder City NV
(800) 875-9348 or (702) 759-3483
www.skydivelasvegas.com

Awesome Adventures

Awesome Adventures specializes in unusual and exciting tours that explore the land and water surrounding Las Vegas. You can tour Red Rock or Eldorado Canyons in rugged, military-style Hummers. Try horseback riding in Red Rock Canyon, where you'll see southwestern desert wildlife and the famous Joshua trees. Kick up a little sand on an ATV tour just outside the Valley of Fire, or take a mountain bike tour through the Valley of Fire State Park. You can discover Lake Mead's hidden coves and secluded beaches on a Sea-Doo two-person watercraft, or sit in a kayak or canoe at the base of Hoover Dam and look all the way up. All tours include a professional guide, hotel pickup and return, bottled water and a meal. Guides are certified in first aid/CPR and by the All-Terrain Vehicle Safety Institute and Tread Lightly. Stoney Ward, owner of Awesome Adventures, started out doing Jet Ski tours of Lake Mead. Later, he became a manager at one of the area marinas. He fell in love with the Valley of Fire and wanted to share the beautiful desert landscape with others. A pioneer of the adventure tour concept, Stoney started Awesome Adventures in 1995. Book your tour and see why businesses from hotels to brokerage companies bring their staff on an Awesome Adventures tour. You'll see the wild side of Nevada and have the experience of a lifetime.

Las Vegas NV
(800) 519-2243
www.adventureseekers.info

Boulder City Outfitters

If you think of Las Vegas when you think of Nevada, perhaps it's time you discovered the rest of Nevada. Boulder City Outfitters started out more than 14 year ago as a kayak rental business, and although it still offers kayak, canoe and bike rentals, owner Bill Pedersen saw a need for guided tours as well. For the past five years Boulder City has featured four types of tours that include kayaking, hiking, mountain biking and ATV trips, with 200 boats, 40 mountain bikes and 20 ATVs available. Many local folks and professional groups return every year. Internationally famous for its kayaking trips, Boulder City Outfitters offers a full day's paddling on the Colorado River through Black Canyon. Launched from the base of Hoover Dam, the trip features spectacular scenery and a chance to soak in hot springs and explore Sauna Cave. You'll have fun with knowledgeable guides who will teach you about the history, flora and fauna of the area while ensuring a safe trip. Try mountain biking through scenic Bootleg Canyon or cruise through the Mojave Desert on an ATV. You can hike the beautiful River Mountain Trail and take in spectacular views of Lake Mead, Boulder City and Las Vegas. For an exciting outdoor experience that combines education, safety and preservation with just plain fun, book your adventure with Boulder City Outfitters.

**1631 Industrial Road, Boulder City NV
(702) 293-1190 or (800) 748-3702**
www.bouldercityoutfitters.com

Julie Anne's Bakery–Café–Fine Foods

Food is a passion at Julie Anne's Bakery–Café–Fine Foods in Henderson with a bakery, a restaurant and a retail shop all centered on special food. The owners thrive on challenging themselves to produce great food choices for their customers, including the Best Chocolate Brownie Ever. The Green Apple Wrap and Cobb Club have a loyal following, and you can ask for samples. Julie Anne Hession and her husband, Eric, will tailor foods to meet their customer's needs, including customized cakes and catering options for weddings, birthdays and special occasions. You can choose from breakfast foods, sandwiches, salads and specialty desserts. Enjoy the convenience of the Gourmet-To-Go dinners; simply call ahead to pick up the daily entrée or casserole. Nightly specials change every other month and are an affordable way to indulge in gourmet fare. Julie Anne's even offers themed gift baskets filled with specialty food items. Bring the kids and let them mix and match by selecting one of the gourmet peanut butter flavors and their own choice of jam. You'll find boxed breakfast or lunch platters and homemade granola that's a big hit in local households. For food every which way you could want it, visit Julie Anne's Bakery–Café–Fine Foods

10895 Eastern Avenue, Henderson NV
(702) 566-9979
www.julieannes.com

India Oven

From the bustling streets of Bombay to the compelling culture of Calcutta, India teams with tantalizing dishes and fascinating combinations of spices and herbs. India Oven brings the fragrant, spicy food of India to your table. *Las Vegas Review-Journal* named the restaurant Best of Las Vegas for six consecutive years, and local reviewers have high praise for India Oven, the creation of 14-year husband and wife team Jitu and Tayshree Patel. You'll enjoy an inviting dining room and a menu that is both extensive and eclectic, offering just about anything one could hope to find in Indian cuisine. The restaurant features a vast array of tandoori specialties, which employ a clay charcoal oven. Chicken *tikka* involves baking small pieces of marinated chicken in the oven. The restaurant also uses the oven to prepare shrimp and *barra kabab*, which is rack of lamb marinated in yogurt and spices. No Indian meal would be complete without the traditional and delectable *naan* bread, created by slapping the dough on the inside walls of the tandoor oven. India Oven offers several delightful versions of *naan*, so you can try it topped with garlic or cheese or stuffed with minced lamb and spices. Whether you prefer poultry, seafood or vegetarian food, spicy or mild fare, India Oven can satisfy your inclinations. You could travel to India or savor authentic tastes from this land of flavorful mysteries without leaving Las Vegas with a visit to India Oven.

2218 Paradise Road, Las Vegas, NV
(702) 366-0222
www.indiaovenlasvegas.com

Kennedy Restaurant & Lounge

Kennedy Restaurant & Lounge, located in the Green Valley Ranch District, caters to the metropolitan lifestyle with an upscale yet casual vibe. Locally owned by Adam Corrigan, tennis star Andre Agassi, Tom Breitling, Perry Rogers and Jeff Marquis, this simple, elegant lounge offers comfy chairs and booths that encourage you to stay for hours. Open 24 hours a day, Kennedy serves food from 11 am to 7 am daily. Executive Chef Michael Ingino, who comes originally from Staten Island, N.Y., came to Las Vegas for a wedding and decided to stay. After working for restaurateur Gustav Mauler for four years at Oxo, Bull Shrimp and Spedini, Ingino now oversees lunch, dinner and late-night menus that are designed to bring in local clientele. His modern American offerings include seafood, steaks, pasta, sandwiches, soups and salads. Try the chopped vegetable salad, Ingino's irresistible medley of diced veggies and bacon topped with potato sticks. Evening guests enjoy the ambience of mood lighting and a choice of more than 40 wines, many by the glass. Kennedy caters to local clientele, many of whom are friends as well as loyal customers, and offers a complimentary menu for top gaming customers. For an elegant destination for gaming and dining, come to the Kennedy Restaurant & Lounge.

2235 Village Walk Drive, Suite 141, Henderson NV
(702) 320-8100
www.kennedytavern.com

Sergio's Italian Gardens

In a city known for its outstanding cuisine, Las Vegas has no finer example of delectable, authentic Italian fare than Sergio's Italian Gardens. Proprietors Sergio and Rosele Oriente of Rome say genuine Italian hospitality is in their blood. The dining room is a study in Old World atmosphere and hospitality, a place where both locals and visitors can enjoy an evening piano serenade while reveling in such authentic dishes as *Osso Buco*, the traditional tender veal shank dish, served here with a side of handmade fettuccini. The extensive menu offers many other delights, from appetizers and salads to pastas, seafood and beef dishes. Sergio's has received favorable notice from many sources and is the winner of such prestigious honors as Five Star, Best of the Best, Gold and Recommended Establishment awards. The American Academy of Hospitality Sciences describes Sergio's as the, "finest in its category and classification," and a *Zagat* survey simply calls it "Excellent." With accolades such as these, it is not unusual to see well-known celebrities dining here. The Orientes offer catering and banquet facilities for wedding receptions, birthday parties and other gatherings of up to 120 people. They will even rent out the restaurant itself, when your budget and availability allow it. For the ultimate experience in Italian cuisine, visit Sergio's Italian Gardens, where Old World meets a new era of satisfaction.

1955 E Tropicana Avenue, Las Vegas NV
(702) 739-1544
www.sergiosrestaurant.com

Go Raw Café

It's good to eat things that are alive and raw. That's the wisdom that drives Go Raw Café, a Las Vegas veggie café and juice bar. How different is this restaurant from the norm? You won't find an oven in the kitchen, nor will you find any meat or animal products here. Cooking destroys vital enzymes, resulting in a less healthy product, according to owner Rod O, who runs the restaurant along with his partner, Lu V. Everything here is made largely with fruits, nuts, seeds and grains plus complementary organic oils. From these simple ingredients, Rod and Lu build a surprising array of flavors into their menu. You'll find everything from soups and salads to enchiladas and lasagna. You can even pick up that staple of American cuisine, a pizza, served here on a raw, sprouted buckwheat crust with almond cheese, marinara sauce and walnut sausage. The thirst quenchers are equally healthy and range from a berry smoothie to such exotic combinations as Popeye's Favorite or the Chlorophyll Cocktail. The décor is pretty and the attitude, relaxed. For pure, healthful foods that pack a favorful punch, visit Go Raw Café.

2381 E Windmill Lane, Las Vegas NV
(702) 450-9007
2910 Lake East Drive, Las Vegas NV
(702) 254-5382
www.gorawcafe.com

Piero's Italian Cuisine

It's no secret that Las Vegas has long been a playground for many of the nation's celebrities, but not everyone knows that those same famed faces prefer to dine at Piero's Italian Cuisine. This A-list eatery is owned and operated by Fred Glusman and has been serving incredible Italian cuisine for more than 25 years to some of the city's most famous headliners, including Frank Sinatra, Debbie Reynolds and Wayne Newton. In April 1994, Jerry Lewis sent Glusman a commendation stating, "There is no place like Piero's." Piero's has been featured in *GQ* magazine and served as a set for the movie *Casino*, staring Joe Pesci, Sharon Stone and Robert De Niro. In the film Piero's doubled for the Leaning Tower restaurant, a fictional Italian eatery based on Piero's itself. Glusman's restaurant also made headlines when FBI agents swooped in during the dinner hour to arrest two men suspected of taking part in mob hits. Glusman took the incident in stride, telling the press, "It's not a mobster place. Anybody who is anybody eats at Piero's." The community enjoys this eatery just as much as the throngs of visitors who flock to the city each year, and numerous annual convention dinners take place here. Enjoy an evening of fine dining while surrounded by an ambience unlike anything else Las Vegas has to offer with reservations at Piero's Italian Cuisine.

355 Convention Center Drive, Las Vegas NV
(702) 369-2305

The King and I

The King and I restaurant allows owners Kris and Nicki Bujadham to bring award-winning Thai cuisine to their casual restaurant hidden away inside a strip mall. Nicki welcomes guests warmly to a cozy interior that features Thai artwork mounted on stone walls reminiscent of a wine cellar. Husband Kris loves introducing authentic Thai food straight from the Thai Culinary Institute to tourists and locals. Considering that some customers eat at King and I five times a week, he must be doing something right. The menu features traditional Thai classics, from appetizers, soups and salads to noodles, fried rice, seafood and meat entrées. Customers specify the spiciness of their food, from the mild Coward through Careful to Adventurous and then to fiery Native Thai. Try the Singapore noodles, angel hair rice noodles stir-fried with shrimp, pork, scallions and a touch of curry, or the much-requested *tom kha gai* soup, chicken in cocoanut milk, galangal spice and lime juice. Once you've sampled the food, you'll know why the King and I won the best of Las Vegas in the *Review Journal* reader's poll three times. You could travel halfway across the world to enjoy wonderfully authentic Thai food in a warm and welcoming atmosphere. Instead, you can visit the King and I at any of three locations—it's a much shorter trip.

1107 E Tropicana Avenue, Las Vegas NV (702) 739-8819
2605 Windmill Parkway, Henderson NV (702) 897-1114
2904 Lake East Drive, Las Vegas NV (702) 256-1568
www.usmenuguide.com/kingithai.html

Table 34

Are you looking for creative cuisine and a friendly neighborhood bistro where they know your name? If so, proceed directly to Table 34. Rich wood floors, desert colors and walls adorned with mirrors and contemporary art lend warmth to the elegant interior. The menu, which changes daily, features great breads and imaginative soups such as apple-butternut squash purée and cream of tomato-tarragon. The seafood is always flown in fresh, never frozen. Starters include the house-smoked salmon on a potato galette (buckwheat crêpe) with parsley-shallot cream. Salads, sandwiches and comfort foods such as chicken pot pie and macaroni and cheese gratinée round out the lunch offerings. Lunch or dinner, you can find favorites such as pizza and all-beef meatloaf on the menu. For dinner, try the braised beef pot roast with herb *spaetzel* and Bordelaise sauce. A selection of more than 100 American wines, many from California, complements the cuisine. Be sure to save room for a dessert such as vanilla bean *crème brulée* or banana fritters with warm berry sauce. Table 34 came into existence when Chef Wes Kendrick teamed up with sister and manager Laurie Kendrick to offer imaginative dishes in a casual, hip environment. For generous portions of spectacular cuisine at affordable prices, come to Table 34.

600 E Warm Springs Road, Las Vegas NV
(702) 263-0034
www.usmenuguide.com/table34.html

Milo's Best Cellars

Milo Hurst had just purchased a building in Boulder City. David Rivera worked in retail wine and wanted to open his own wine shop. In 2003, they joined forces to open Milo's Best Cellars, offering a few appetizers and cheeses to complement their wines. Eventually their customers asked for more variety, and Milo's Best Cellars became a bistro as well as a wine shop. Milo and David created the menu for the restaurant together. David, the sommelier, likes to choose wines that are good values, and most of the wines offered are between $10 and $25 per bottle. He brings in 10 to 15 new varieties at restocking time, thus offering a wider selection of wines than is normally found in casual restaurants. Milo's stocks more than 400 wines and 50 beers from around the world. Milo and David want customers to know that wine is approachable and host a weekly wine tasting with a master sommelier. Customers gravitate to the heated outdoor patio, where they can sip wine in the center of Old Town Boulder City and do some people watching. Vegetarian sandwiches and the Chianti platter are favorites with customers, who also enjoy the large selection of wines by the glass. Come enjoy the laid-back ambience at Milo's Best Cellars and see why the *Las Vegas Mercury* calls the bistro "a unique brand of small-town hip that makes dining at Milo's a mini-vacation."

538 Nevada Way, Boulder City NV
(702) 293-9540
www.miloswinebar.com

Golden Steer Steak House

Since 1958, the Golden Steer Steak House has served both the famous and infamous. Private dining booths, outstanding service and generous, perfectly broiled steaks have attracted such celebrities as Frank Sinatra, Sammy Davis, Jr., Marilyn Monroe, Elvis Presley and Anthony "Tony the Ant" Spilotro. Prominently located one block west of Las Vegas Boulevard on Sahara Avenue, this five-star restaurant is a true icon of classic Las Vegas. Proprietors Dr. Michael J. Signorelli and Don and Alice Lynwalter continue the tradition by preserving the Golden Steer's original crooners atmosphere. You can slip into a roomy red leather booth in one of the restaurant's intimate dining areas and enjoy prime beef, double cut lamb chops or Western Australian lobster tails. The service offered by the Golden Steer's professional staff adds to the enjoyment of any meal here. The Golden Steer's seductive piano bar beckons diners for before or after-dinner drinks with classic Fifties music. Crowds are as comfortable as couples at the Golden Steer, where large, plush dining areas serve parties of 20 or more. For the feel and flavor of Old Vegas, come to the Golden Steer Steak House. You just might see one of today's celebrities in the booth next to yours.

308 W Sahara Avenue, Las Vegas NV
(702) 384-4470
www.goldensteerlv.com

Todd's Unique Dining

At Todd's Unique Dining in Henderson, *unique* is not just a name. "By calling us *unique*, it gives me a palette for changing the menu," says Todd Clore, who opened the casual yet elegant restaurant in May 2004 with his wife, Terry. Creative contemporary cuisine is a priority here, and Todd wants his customers to try food that may be "out of their realm." "When you have fish at our restaurant, I can guarantee that it'll be fresh and in season," Todd says. Seafood is flown in daily from places like Cape Cod and Alaska and is only a few hours old when it arrives at Todd's. Choose seafood or consider the popular braised Kobe boneless short ribs with jalapeño mashed potatoes and crisp onions. Specials change often depending on what is fresh and what creative twist Todd has in mind. Round out your meal with a drink from the full-service bar with its extensive wine list. Todd's can also cater your next event. Todd's inspiration comes from his varied experiences as a chef in Denver, Napa Valley and Los Angeles. He is a graduate of the Culinary Institute of America, and his work has been featured on the Travel Channel and Food Channel as well as in *Gourmet* magazine. He was *Las Vegas Life* magazine's Epicurean award winner. Treat your palate at Todd's Unique Dining and taste *unique* for yourself.

4350 E Sunset Road, Henderson NV
(702) 259-TODD (8633)
www.toddsunique.com

Roma Deli, Restaurant and More Than Bread Bakery

Giuseppe Consarino promises guests the most authentic Italian experience in the area when they eat at Roma Deli, Restaurant and More Than Bread Bakery. Giuseppe and his crew uphold high standards for his establishment by making their own sausage, mozzarella and many more Italian specialties. The restaurant is open everyday for lunch and dinner, featuring the cuisine of Angelina Catania, an Italian homemaker from Sicily. The restaurant is decorated like a restaurant you'd find in Italy. Roma Deli is the place for everything, from deli meats, olive oils, fresh bread, eggplant parmigiana to Braciola, which is thinly sliced beef rolled with provolone, raisins and pine nuts and slowly baked in the oven. The breads at Roma Deli come from More Than Bread, Giuseppe's wholesale bakery. More Than Bread produces over 200 types of artisan breads, pastries and cakes for popular restaurants and hotels throughout Las Vegas, including such famous ones as Bertolini's, Stratosphere, Bellagio and the Mandalay Bay. "If you've been through Las Vegas," Giuseppe says, "then you've eaten something from More Than Bread." Indeed, no culinary tour is complete without sampling how Las Vegas does Italian. To eat in Las Vegas as they do in Rome, choose Roma Deli, Restaurant and More Than Bread Bakery located inside the Sienna Plaza.

5755 Spring Mountain Road, Las Vegas NV
(702) 871-5577
www.MoreThanBread.com

Alizé at the Top of the Palms

You'll find plenty of reasons to make Alizé at the Top of the Palms your destination for dining when you are in Las Vegas. Located at the top of the Palms Casino Resort, world-class cuisine here comes with a 280-degree view of the city from 16-foot floor-to-ceiling windows. The brainchild of owner and proprietor Chef André Rochat, Alizé is the crown jewel in André's Las Vegas culinary empire, joining the respected André's French Restaurant and Andre's in the Monte Carlo Casino Resort. Tables are generously spaced, and the atmosphere is modern and elegant. With dozens of cold and hot appetizer choices, deciding where to start will be your first dilemma. Will it be the caviar followed by the pepper-crusted filet mignon or the stuffed portobello mushrooms followed by sautéed duck? Of course, the biggest decision will come in choosing your wine from the two-story glass wine cellar right in the middle of the restaurant, home to 5,000 bottles and the largest selection of Cognac around. Named one of the top new restaurants in the world in 2003 by *Conde Nast Traveler* magazine, this AAA Four Diamond winner makes an ideal setting for a business meeting or a romantic dinner for two. André has named Alizé at the Top of the Palms after the gentle trade winds that sweep the French Caribbean Islands. Come let the fine dining and dramatic views of the famed Las Vegas strip sweep you away.

4321 W Flamingo Road, Las Vegas NV
(702) 951-7000
www.alizelv.com

Chicago Brewing Company

Chicago Brewing Company is located inside of a 9,000-square-foot brick warehouse with sky-high ceilings and stained glass all around. Glass panels are the only barrier between you and the large copper brew kettles that work 24/7 to produce some of the finest beers you have tasted. Brewmaster Kyle Cormier's goal is to brew 1,200 barrels of beer per year. That's 2,300 cases or 30,000 gallons. Kyle achieves his goal with perfection, producing World Beer Cup gold-medal winners such as the Belgian Dubbel. Chicago Brewing offers seven different beers on tap, depending on the season, including Ramblin' Reck Amber Ale, Old Town Brown (another medal winner), and their aggressively hopped Hardaway I.P.A. In addition to great beer, Chicago Brewing serves tasty food with a Chicago theme. You'll find baby back ribs soaked in Old Town Brown. The Black Star Ribeye is marinated in, you guessed it, Black Star Stout. They make a true Chicago-style deep-dish pizza here, too. Chicago Brewing Company creates the perfect environment for you to relax, have a great meal and great beer. The next time you're in Las Vegas, visit Chicago Brewing Company and taste how hops were meant to be used.

2201 Fort Apache, Las Vegas NV
(702) 254-3333
www.chicagobrewingcolv.com

The Bagel Café

If you're looking for an unexpected taste of New York City in Las Vegas, the Bagel Café, a bakery and a deli restaurant, should be your first stop. Open for breakfast, lunch and dinner, the café's expansive menu includes sandwiches served cold, hot and grilled, plus soups, salads, pizza and fish. The deliciously chewy bagels are standouts, as are an assortment of tempting baked goods. Owner Savvas Andrews came to America from Cyprus in 1980 with $100 in his pocket and a few words of English in his vocabulary. Dreaming of someday owning his own business, he went to school in New York City while working in Greek diners. Today Savvas and his wife, Shari, run a thriving business, where you are likely to spot priests, rabbis and such celebrities as Andre Agassi, Steffi Graf and the mayor of Las Vegas. This one-of-a-kind mom and pop shop is a *Las Vegas Review Journal* Best of Las Vegas winner, and the walls are lined with awards and framed articles about the café, as well as photos of celebrities spotted having lunch here. The family-friendly eatery draws scads of local folks too, and about half of the café's business comes from take-out orders. If you're planning a special occasion, relax and let the Bagel Café cater your event. From matzo ball soup and stuffed cabbage to fabulous pastries and gourmet coffee, when you want mouthwatering food, turn to the Bagel Café.

301 N Buffalo Drive, Las Vegas NV
(702) 255-3444
www.thebagelcafelv.com

M & M's Soul Food

M & M's Soul Food restaurant brings Mississippi home cooking to the glamorous Las Vegas. Founded in Los Angeles in the late 1960s by Mary Stewart (also known as Mississippi Mary), this restaurant has been serving the Las Vegas community for over half a decade. The menu includes southern favorites such as fried chicken, chitterlings, catfish, greens, yams and macaroni and cheese. A friendly atmosphere welcomes you with the sounds of rhythm and blues playing in the background, which adds to the southern home-cooking experience. M & M's has received numerous awards including Best Soul Food Restaurant in Las Vegas 2002, 2003, 2004, 2006 and 2007. The guest list includes B. B. King, George Wallace, Rudy Ray Moore and world champion fighters Winky Wright, Leila Ali, Floyd Mayweather Jr. and Bernadette Stanis. So come have a good time with Tim G. and his staff on the corner of Charleston and Valley View for an unforgettable experience.

3923 W Charleston Blvd, Las Vegas NV
(702) 453-7685
www.mmsoulfoodcafe.com

Black Mountain Grill

Green Mountain's Black Mountain Grill offers upscale dining and gaming in a rustic lodge environment. Proprietor Donna Rocker, a former resident of both Oregon and Maine, uses stone walls and high beamed ceilings to create an elegant environment. Customers can watch the chefs at work in the exhibition kitchen, relax near the fireplace or dine on the mezzanine. An outdoor patio and fountain add to Black Mountain's charms. Cuisine here marries the American Pacific rim with Asian influences, creating a fusion of tantalizing flavors that encompasses breakfast, lunch and dinner. A popular starter is the pancetta-wrapped prawns with a Thai barbecue sauce. Other appetizers include the baked spinach and portobello dip or the cilantro lime buffalo wings. Main courses are equally diverse and include such delights as Chilean sea bass served with Asian vegetables, herb roasted chicken, filet mignon or gourmet pizzas. Meals at Black Mountain are as much about presentation as flavor. The grill offers a selection of microbrews large enough for you to find just the right selection to complement any meal on the menu. If you are planning a private party, General Manager Matthew J. Urso can offer one of two private dining rooms, including a loft. For beautiful surroundings, open for eating or gambling 24 hours a day, visit Black Mountain Grill.

11021 S Eastern Avenue, Henderson NV
(702) 990-0990
www.blackmountaingrill.com

Wild Truffles Gourmet Café

Owners Eva and Georg Paulussen and their son Daniel came together to open Wild Truffles Gourmet Café. Both Eva and Georg are chefs in their own right, and have worked in some of the greatest cities in the world, including New Delhi, New York, New Jersey, Boston, London and Tokyo. Prior to opening Wild Truffles in Las Vegas, Georg was the Vice President of Culinary Operations at the Atlantis Resort & Casino. Before that he was the opening Executive Chef for the Venetian Resort & Casino in Las Vegas. Wild Truffles is open for continental breakfast, lunch, dinner and brunch on Sundays. The menu reflects that of a European bistro with fine dining cuisine served in a casual setting. Some starters on the menu include watermelon and pineapple with fried goat cheese, or crab and lobster cake with avocado. Entrées offer an international flavor with jerk marinated lamb chops, rare tuna *tataki* and *tandoori* crusted chicken breast. The menu boasts a large selection of sandwiches on fresh baked artisan breads, salads, gelato (a European sweet treat), and an enhanced coffee service. Guests can enjoy a taste of international and domestic cheese as they sip on their wine. You can also take home fresh chocolate dipped strawberries as well as many other fruits, and a wide selection of truffles and pralines presented in unusual keepsake vessels such as leather trunks, suitcases and wooden trains. This form of presentation and content is by far not usual in the gift basket arena. If you need to serve a crowd be sure to ask about the box lunch options, which can be prepared in orders from one to thousands. Chef Georg has been featured on the Discovery Channel and the Travel Channel. For high-end casual dining without setting foot in a casino, visit Wild Truffles Gourmet Café.

750 S Rampart Boulevard, Suite #7, Las Vegas NV (702) 938- 8803 *www.wild-truffles.com*

Firefly* on Paradise

Firefly* on Paradise is a remarkable tapas kitchen & bar. In case you're unfamiliar with tapas, think of what the French refer to as hors d'oeuvres, what the Chinese call dim sum, and what the Italians call antipasto. The Spanish call these little treasures tapas, but unlike their cousins around the world, tapas are more than just appetizers. The ingredients that go into the making of Spanish tapas are limited only by a chef's imagination. You can try two or three as a snack, or order several at once to create a delicious meal. Firefly* owner and chef John Simmons will tantalize your every taste bud with a variety of tapas that take you from Spain to Japan and everywhere in between, including *camarones a la diabla*, crispy duck rolls, and bacon wrapped dates, to name but a few. Need something substantial in front of you? Try the paella or the steak frites with a 14-ounce ribeye. John's goal is to provide a great meal in a cool restaurant at an economical price. Firefly* is open till 2 am Monday through Friday and until 3 am on the weekend. Music starts at 10:30 with Doug Gibbs and Jason Lema offering you a midnight snack of down-tempo funk, old school tunes, or salsa and meringue. Whether you are in Spain or at Firefly* on Paradise, tapas go hand-in-hand with hospitality, friendship, sangria and music. Live the tradition and see why both *Citysearch* and the *Las Vegas Review-Journal* voted Firefly* the best of Las Vegas.

3900 Paradise Road Suite A, Las Vegas NV
(702) 369-3971
www.fireflylv.com

Settebello

Brad Otton, a former USC quarterback, learned about pizza when he spent two years in Italy on a mission for his church. After returning to Naples in 2004 for formal training, Brad opened Settebello Pizzeria Napoletana, named for the luckiest card in the Italian card game of Scopa. Settebello is one of only 15 pizzerias in the United States–and the only one in Nevada–that's certified to conform to stringent standards of VPN, an Italian-language acronym for real Neapolitan pizza. To earn this designation, pizza must be cooked on the floor of a wood-fired oven, and the dough must be hand worked. Brad uses only fresh mozzarella, imported Parmigiano-Reggiano cheese and Italian tomatoes that he imports from San Marzano, Italy, so that they're grown on volcanic soil. He also imported Carmine D'Amato, an authentic Italian *pizzaiolo*, or pizza maker. His fabulous pizzas boast a thin crust with smoky flavor and a good balance of cheese, sauce and cured or cooked prosciutto (ham), pancetta (bacon), Italian anchovies, salame (salami), roasted vegetables or wood-oven sausage. You won't find pepperoni or Canadian bacon on the menu, though, and pizzas are served uncut unless a customer requests a sliced pizza. To experience authentic Napoli pizza as it was made in Naples in the 1700s, directly from the oven, with a crisp, bubbly crust that you tear apart with your fingers, come to Settebello.

1776 Horizon Ridge Parkway, Henderson NV
(702) 222-3556
www.settebello.net

Andre's Las Vegas

The food critic who claimed that André Rochat has earned "a place in the pantheon of Las Vegas' most celebrated chefs" is not alone in his praise. All who visit Andre's Restaurant know that they are in for a fine dining experience with an absolute master. While trends come and go, André keeps tradition alive with such dishes as rack of lamb, Dover sole and a duck breast with green peppercorn plum sauce. "So many classic dishes have been forgotten because so many young chefs don't know enough about basic cooking," says André, whose opinions may be old school but endear him to his many loyal fans. "Whatever is on the plate has to have a reason to be on the plate," he continues. "It has to enhance the main ingredient." Andre's Restaurant is located in a former residential neighborhood in downtown Las Vegas and was, indeed, built as a house in the 1930s. Its cozy rooms and French country décor feel like a house in the little village in the French Alps where André was born and raised. André opened his first restaurant in 1980 and went on to open the elegant André's at the Monte Carlo in 1997 and Alizé on top of the Palms Casino Resort in 2001. For classic French cuisine from a master, visit Andre's Restaurant.

401 S 6ᵗʰ Street, Las Vegas NV
(702) 385-5016
www.andrelv.com

Prime Time Meat Market

In a city that prides itself on $1.99 all-you-can-eat buffets, it was pretty challenging to find great cuts of meat for home preparation until David LeFevre opened the Prime Time Meat Market in Henderson in 2003. David first came to Las Vegas on vacation and saw an opportunity to build a successful business in the meat industry, his area of expertise for 10 years. David and his Shop Manager Angela Haven provide their customers with top-quality meats and seafoods, shipped daily from the world's best producers. You'll also discover such exotic game as buffalo, kangaroo and alligator. Prime Time offers its own house-brand seasonings and tender beef jerky, made from the same prime, dry-aged beef stocked in the display cases. The market further carries pre-marinated cuts of beef and seafood for easy preparation at home. Prime Cut's delivery service makes stocking your freezer a snap. While it would be fun to try, you can't live on meat alone, so Prime Time makes your after-work shopping a breeze with a full selection of fresh produce, sliced deli meats and delicious cheeses, as well as selected boxed goods for your convenience. Skip the glitz of the downtown eateries, drive on by the grocery store, and get what you need to enjoy a quiet meal at home with quality meats and all the trimmings from Prime Time Meat Market.

1550 Horizon Ridge Parkway, Henderson NV
(702) 492-9998
www.lvmeat.com

Periwinkle Cottage

Periwinkle Cottage provides retail sales treasures to women in Southern Nevada. It's owner, Karen Pellouchoud was named Boulder City Business Person of the Year in 2006. What is all the buzz about? Periwinkle Cottage gives people an experience in shopping that is not available anywhere else, including larger stores and name-brand shops. Women love Karen and her store. At Periwinkle, shoppers browse finest quality goods including bath and body products, French soaps and products from market leaders such as Vera Bradley, Demdaco and Evelyn-Crabtree. This shop has helped energize retail sales businesses throughout the Boulder City Historic District. The excitement becomes feverish over the large selection of Mary Frances purses in dazzling displays at Periwinkle Cottage. Oprah Winfrey and Jennifer Aniston are just two of the celebrities that own Mary Frances purses. These purses are so popular at Periwinkle Cottage that Karen founded a purse club and invited Mary Frances herself to breakfast at the historic Boulder Dam Hotel. Mary Frances personally signed purses owned by the 80 proud ladies who attended. Experience Periwinkle Cottage. You might just find yourself joining the Mary Frances purse club.

503 Hotel Plaza, Boulder City NV
(702) 293-5767
www.periwinklebc.com

Celebrating 30 years in Las Vegas

The Jewelers of Las Vegas

The Jewelers of Las Vegas is family owned and operated, and it is also one of the largest jewelry businesses in Nevada. Owner Mordechai Yerushalmi was born in Israel and settled in Las Vegas in 1973. His career is a classic American success story. "Buy right, manufacture right and provide quality and service, and you'll succeed," Mordechai says. In fact, Mordechai and his staff handcrafted much of the jewelry on display at The Jewelers' unpretentious flagship showroom on Western Avenue. The Jewelers has several other stores in Las Vegas, including locations at many of the most famous resorts on the Strip, such as Caesars Palace, Paris Las Vegas, the Venetian and Mandalay Place. The Jewelers is world famous because of its work for celebrities and sports figures. Mordechai began by making jewelry for such Vegas-based performers as Wayne Newton and Liberace. He made Liberace's original piano ring. The list of Hollywood stars, singers and boxers that Mordechai has served over the years seems endless. The Jewelers' bread-and-butter customers, however, are average Americans enjoying themselves in Las Vegas. At The Jewelers, you can find that special surprise gift or ask the shop to create a dream piece of your very own. The *Nevada Business Journal* has voted The Jewelers of Las Vegas the number-one jewelry store in town. Enjoy some of the sparkle discovered by the stars with a visit to The Jewelers of Las Vegas.

2400 Western Avenue, Las Vegas NV (702) 382-7411 *www.thejewelers.com*

Las Vegas Paper Doll

With stationery, Las Vegas-centric cards and many other paper products, Las Vegas Paper Doll has everything you need to Do the Write Thing. Owner Anne Kellogg, with previous careers in public relations and journalism, has been an advocate of paper and the printed word for most of her life. Las Vegas Paper Doll offers a return to the comfy correspondence of pen and paper as opposed to the abstract, digital e-mails and instant messages so common in today's world. You'll find greeting cards here for every occasion, including one-of-a-kind gohgirl cards from Liz Goh and the satirical greeting cards and postcards of photographer Jonnie Andersen that poke fun at the glitz and glamour of Vegas. Kellogg displays her cards creatively. Some are even framed and changed occasionally as if they were pieces in an art gallery. "I try to show people that they don't have to be intimidated by the arts, and we provide products with an artsy focus," she says. The store also offers specialty printing for invitations and personalized stationery as well as gift items and publications from local publishers. If you're looking for the perfect paper for your pen pal, come to Las Vegas Paper Doll.

**231 W Charleston Boulevard, Suite 120, Las Vegas NV
(in the Holsum Design Center building)
(702) 385-7892**
www.lvpaperdoll.com

Flights of Fancy

Flights of Fancy is a unique place where you can find wind toys for kids of all ages. From kites and windsocks to spinners, Frisbees and boomerangs, Flights of Fancy carries kinetic devices that are fun and add movement to your yard or garden. Flights of Fancy was started by Jim Hodge, a physicist, and Lori Jo Klemptner, an engineer, who wanted to bring a kite and wind-related store to the Las Vegas area. With two locations, Jim and Lori have created a concept that is very hard to categorize. It is a toy store, yet it is also a garden décor center. It is a kite store, but it is also a place to spice up your home. Whether you are looking for kites or a unique kinetic decoration to accent your garden, you can find it here. They feature spinners, banners, hand-tuned wind chimes and a wide variety of decorative items not found anyplace else. You'll find hanging leaded crystals, Soleri bells, hand-blown radiometers, decorative orbs and mobiles of every type. You've really got to see their selection to appreciate it. Visit Flights of Fancy next time you're in the Las Vegas area. You won't be able to leave without buying something fun.

**20 Costa di Lago, Suite 130, Henderson NV
(MonteLago Village) (702) 558-6202
120 S Green Valley Parkway, Suite 154, Henderson NV
(Green Valley Ranch) (702) 736-7771**
www.flightsoffancylv.com

Fabreana

The store logo of a red high heel suggests that Fabreana is the place for shoes, shoes and more shoes. When you step through the door and gaze upon all of the beautiful footwear, you'll know that the logo speaks the truth. Shop for sturdy walking shoes or gardening clogs elsewhere. Fabreana carries the kind of footwear that draws attention—open-toe pumps, beaded sandals, thongs and round-toe ankle boots. While shoes are the main attraction, Fabreana also carries high quality but reasonably priced accessories. Credit the women of Fabreana with making the most of a small space. The boutique may be a nook, but the selection is superb, and the space never feels cramped. The mother and daughter team of Anna and Regina Schrieffer bring it all together in a shop that's a style statement itself. Clusters of shoes, necklaces and bags adorn tiered tabletops. Belts of various colors and textures are draped across the backs of chairs and couches. It all looks so gorgeous that you'll want to take a picture. Regina cites customer service as her top priority. She recalls the day when her father sent her on a shopping trip to buy some expensive jewelry for her mother. Because she happened to be wearing sweats and flip-flops, no salesperson would pay attention to her, even though she was ready to make their day. "You don't have to dress up to shop at Fabreana," says Regina. Save the head-turning look for the evening when you wear the shoes and carry the handbag that you bought at this sharp boutique.

8000 W Sahara Avenue, Suite 150, Las Vegas NV
(702) 363-2555
www.fabreana.com

If The Shoe Fits...

Looking for fun, fashionable shoes, handbags and accessories, plus personalized service that goes beyond what you'll find in most stores? At If The Shoe Fits, Michelle Merhi and Deanna Yeates offer fashionable ladies shoes, stylish bags and trendy accessories that allow customers to express their own personalities. Michelle and Deanna say a typical customer remark is, "Wow, you have so many different and unique things that you can't find at any other store." Deanna learned the ins and outs of buying fashion merchandise during almost two decades with a large retail company, and Michelle has spent more than a decade in the retail fashion and home décor industry. They teamed up in 2005 to offer the personal touch and convenience of a small boutique. Focusing on great customer service, Michelle and Deanna often help customers put together an entire outfit, assisting them in developing their own individual style. If The Shoe Fits features shoes by Onex, Diego Di Lucca, Moda Spana, Matisse, J.Renee and Chinese Laundry, among many other name brands. An extensive selection of accessories includes handbags from Guess, Kathy Van Zeeland and Mary Frances to name a few. An eclectic array of jewelry provides the sparkling finishing touch. Stop by and visit If The Shoe Fits and step out in style.

10624 S Eastern Avenue, Suite C, Henderson NV
(702) 641-7463

Tesoro Trading Company

When Montelago Village approached Marianne and Harry Freeman about opening a gift store, the Freemans eagerly accepted the offer to share their passion for beautiful handcrafted items discovered during their travels to Mexico and launched the Tesoro Trading Company retail store in Henderson in 2003. *Tesoro* means *treasure* in Spanish, and Marianne and Harry have filled their store with treasures of furnishings, jewelry, artwork and ceramics. The store evokes an Old World Spanish Colonial feel and includes exquisite handmade items from several states in central Mexico, including Jalisco, Guanajuato and Querétaro. Unusual jewelry fashioned from semiprecious stones and silver grace the display areas, and furniture and accessories handcrafted by Mexican artisans lend an heirloom look to the store's interior. Tesoro's artwork evinces a more global feel, and the owners, who have over 20 years of experience in the picture framing industry, frame all artwork. The Freemans recently framed more than 100 paintings for actor Tony Curtis and can create a variety of custom looks to suit your décor. You'll enjoy browsing Tesoro's mezzanine level, which contains additional artwork. Whether you're looking for a five-foot-tall candle or a handcrafted wrought iron bench, come to Tesoro Trading Company for gifts, furniture and accessories that showcase the history and artistry of Mexico.

25 Viaduct Bel Canto, Henderson NV
(702) 567-0891
www.tesorotradingco.com

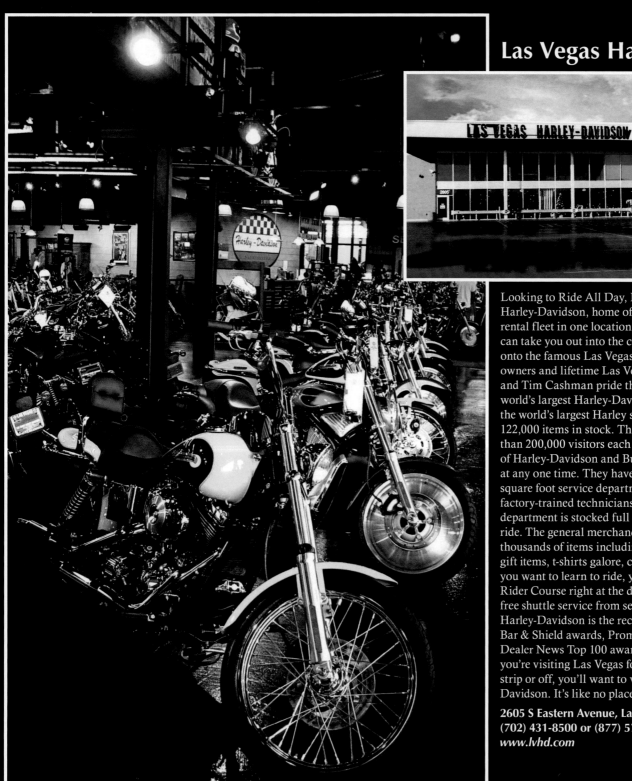

Las Vegas Harley-Davidson

Looking to Ride All Day, Play All Night? Las Vegas Harley-Davidson, home of the largest Harley-Davidson rental fleet in one location, rents motorcycles that can take you out into the countryside by day and onto the famous Las Vegas Strip at night. Current owners and lifetime Las Vegas residents Don Andress and Tim Cashman pride themselves on owning the world's largest Harley-Davidson dealership, featuring the world's largest Harley selection and more than 122,000 items in stock. This dealership serves more than 200,000 visitors each year with more than 500 of Harley-Davidson and Buell motorcycles for sale at any one time. They have an expansive 27,000 square foot service department that has master level, factory-trained technicians. The parts and accessories department is stocked full of items to customize your ride. The general merchandise department carries thousands of items including leather for all riding needs, gift items, t-shirts galore, children's items and more. If you want to learn to ride, you can take the Rider's Edge Rider Course right at the dealership. They also offer free shuttle service from select strip hotels. Las Vegas Harley-Davidson is the recipient of several prestigious Bar & Shield awards, Promoter of the Year awards, Dealer News Top 100 awards and more. Whether you're visiting Las Vegas for all it has to offer on the strip or off, you'll want to visit Las Vegas Harley-Davidson. It's like no place you'll ever experience.

2605 S Eastern Avenue, Las Vegas NV
(702) 431-8500 or (877) 571-7174
www.lvhd.com

Novel Designs
Executive Gift Service

Three words—upscale, sophisticated and innovative—best describe this Las Vegas-based gift basket company. Novel Designs Executive Gift Service specializes in the art of creating modern gift baskets for everyday occasions and corporate events. With a no-wicker-allowed policy, Novel Designs' artful arrangements begin with contemporary yet functional containers. Containers can range anywhere from car consoles and sleek silver ice bins to hand-painted wooden toy boxes and designer handbags. The creative choices are unlimited. Owner Kathi Behrens hand-selects the superior-quality assortment of premium gourmet snacks, fresh fruit, award-winning chocolates, five-star rated bath and spa essentials, upscale gift items and more. The finished presentation is always stylish and sophisticated. Novel Designs also offers an exclusive line of professionally gift-wrapped baskets, corporate discounts, dependable delivery service, personal shopping, complimentary consultations and other innovative gifting solutions. Whatever your needs, Novel Designs will make your gift giving experience exciting and stress free. Novel Designs Executive Gift Service serves Las Vegas, Henderson, Green Valley, Summerlin and Boulder City.

Las Vegas NV
(702) 480-5540
www.noveldesignsllc.com

Little Divas…It's a Girl Thing

Little Divas…It's a Girl Thing specializes in treats for little girls, from huggable Gund stuffed animals to frilly hair accessories and jewelry. Judy Palmer and Genevieve Carrasco opened their fun and festive shop in 2006 based on the concept of Anything a Girl Wants. From the moment they step inside, wide-eyed little girls fall in love with the happy fuchsia, deep purple, gold and dark lime color scheme. Although the shop offers everything from hot-pink digital cameras to feminine bedroom doors, Little Divas specializes in memorable birthday bashes. The open yet separate party area allows parents to relax and watch while the girls enjoy two hours of creative dress-up. Birthday packages include a choice of costumes: rock star, movie star or princess. Each girl receives a Little Divas backpack with lotion and matching body wash in bubble-gum scents and either hair accessories or a bracelet. Karaoke and dancing, hair design and nail polishing complete the royal treatment, and the birthday girl receives a framed photograph of herself with her friends at the end of the festivities. Whether you're looking for dance apparel, costumes or crystal jewelry for mom and daughter, you'll find it at Little Divas. While you're there, be sure to book your princess's next birthday party.

9330 W Sahara Avenue, Suite 130, Las Vegas NV
(702) 341-9003

T-Bird Jewels

T-Bird Jewels has been a Las Vegas tradition for over 40 years and offers a selection of fine quality jewelry and Swiss timepieces. Mickey Kulwin first opened the doors of T-Bird Jewels in 1962 at the legendary Thunderbird Hotel. A cadre of famous faces including the King of Rock and Roll, Elvis Presley, have walked through the doors. Over the years, T-Bird Jewels has designed jewelry for some of the nation's most beloved stars including Jerry Lewis, Sammy Davis, and the elaborately bejeweled Liberace. Although the Thunderbird Hotel is now a nostalgic Las Vegas memory, T-Bird Jewels still maintains the standards of days gone by. Today, Mickey's son Darryl has taken the business to the next level. As Las Vegas has grown, Darryl saw the need to locate his upscale concept in Las Vegas residential areas. There are two convenient locations, one in Summerlin's Trails Village Center and the other in The District in Henderson. T-Bird Jewels carries designer jewelry lines such as Simon G, Jeff Cooper, Michael B, David Yurman and Roberto Coin. Swiss timepieces are represented by Rolex, Cartier, Breitling and Baum Mercier. Take time to indulge yourself in the star treatment you receive a T-Bird Jewels.

1990 Village Center Circle, Las Vegas NV (Trails Village Center) (702) 256-3900
120 S Green Valley Parkway, Henderson NV (The District) (702) 588-5141
www.tbirdjewels.com

Pheasant Cigars

Pheasant Cigars, located one mile from the Las Vegas Strip, offers paradise to the cigar smoker in the form of quality cigars, knowledgeable staff and fair pricing. Brothers Paul Kovacic Jr. and Carl Valentino had already developed an excellent knowledge of cigars from the consumer side of the sales counter before owning this business. So, when the opportunity presented itself, Paul and Carl bought Pheasant Cigars. It is the opinion of many Las Vegas cigar smokers (as well as tourists) that Paul and Carl have developed the finest cigar store in Las Vegas where customer service is always first. Pheasant Cigars maintains one of the largest and best stocked humidors in Nevada. You will discover the finest cigars in the industry including Fuente Opus X, Padron Anniversario & 1926 Serie, Ashton VSG and many others. When you choose membership in the private cigar club you will be welcomed into a smoking lounge furnished in leather and dark woods, an excellent place to relax. The following amenities are available to members: wireless networking, fax machines, USB pluggable printers, gaming tables, 50-inch HDTV, XM Satellite and the finest locker storage system in Nevada. Each locker holds 30 to 50 boxes of cigars and has a separate temperature and humidity control. There are 56 lockers that are all appointed in Spanish cedar and Honduran mahogany. Come and join Paul and Carl for a cigar at Pheasant Cigars. We are certain you'll love the experience.

2800 W Sahara Avenue, Suite 6A, Las Vegas NV (702) 368-1700 *www.pheasantcigars.com*

Jewelry & Mineral of Las Vegas

In a city known for dazzle, Jean Pierre Piron's Jewelry & Mineral of Las Vegas shines bright with one of the most mind-boggling displays of minerals, gems, beads and crystals in existence. One of the last true Indiana Jones-style traders, Belgium-born Jean Pierre left a lengthy career in the aviation industry and a home in the Congo to bring exotic items to Las Vegas. Since opening in 1986, Jean Pierre's venture has been captivating locals and tourists with a dizzying display of relics, carvings, ironwood and African art. You'll be mesmerized by room after room of enthralling exhibits harvested from the farthest corners of the earth, such as 1,000-pound crystals and genuine dinosaur fossils. Equally intriguing are the stories of peril and adventure you may hear from the adventurous proprietor himself, a five-time plane crash survivor who has lived more in his one life than most of us would in 10 lives. For vicarious adventure and a captivating collection of rare jewelry and mineral specimens from around the world, stop by Jewelry & Mineral of Las Vegas, a distinctive gem in a city of gleaming treasures.

**410 E Sahara Avenue, Las Vegas NV
(702) 733-7166**

Delaria Bros. Goldsmiths

There is no inventory at Dave and Jeff Delaria's Henderson jewelry shop, just ideas. Customers come to Delaria Brothers Goldsmiths with a notion of what they want. Often someone brings in stones and asks that a jewelry piece be created around them. After listening carefully, Dave works out a computer-aided design that usually stuns clients with how accurately it captures what they have imagined. In this way, jeweler and customer collaborate to discover, design and build a beautiful ring, pendant or bracelet. "We try to make pieces that people will keep in their families forever," says Dave. "We want customers to realize that they have a unique jewelry piece when they leave." With a background in art and design, Dave has been in business with his brother since 1996. Jeff is the expert at repairing and restoring. They both realize that a piece of jewelry is much more than a merely functional object or a simple fashion statement. It's a reflection of the wearer's unique style, taste and personality. The brothers look forward to using their creative flair and artistic talent to create or restore jewelry that sets you apart. Bring your ideas to Dave and Jeff at Delaria Brothers Goldsmiths.

10940 Eastern Avenue, #112, Henderson NV
(702) 837-8100
www.dbgold.com

Lollipops & Roses

Lollipops & Roses is a combination sweet shop, flower shop and gift shop. The inspiration for this combination of delights comes from partners Sherie Koch and Kathi Enns. For 20 years, Sherie has been baking desserts and Kathi has been creating floral arrangements. By putting their expertise together, they created a shop that meets the needs of every gift giver. Sherie is famous for her caramel and white chocolate popcorn and her pumpkin rolls. Kathi can create bouquets to celebrate any occasion as well as all the flower arrangements for a wedding or other special event. The gift shop is well stocked with bath products, baby items, kitchen décor and specialty foods, priced to fit any budget. Kathi and Sherie are hands-on owners and offer personal greetings to every customer who enters their store. Kathi and her daughter, Amanda, do all the creative displays here, making this shop a treat for the eye. Items here lend themselves to gift baskets, and the shop offers pre-made baskets as well as custom creations. Kathi and Sherie can also create party favors for you. You'll have lots of fun browsing through the merchandise assortment and choosing from such sweet indulgences as cookies, brownies, candy, regular and sugar-free chocolate and truffles. Gifts include decorative home accents, garden décor, plants and furniture. Let Lollipops & Roses surprise you with delights to cover life's many gift giving occasions.

3460 E Sunset Road, Suite M, Las Vegas NV
(702) 655-3340
www.lollipopsnroses.com

Houdini's Magic Shop

Geno Munari has been doling out giggles and tricks at Houdini's Magic Shop since 1993. Today, Geno's business has six Vegas locations plus shops in San Francisco, New York, Atlantic City and Irvine, California. Geno and his team have created a collection of quality magic products that are for sale at the shops and on the Houdini Magic website. You'll find a wide range of new and classic magic tricks and sets, along with books, videos, jokes and gag gifts. Houdini's Magic Shop is also a great place to find magic related posters, signs and rare collectibles. The inventory of costumes and masks will make any magicians' show complete. Houdini's Magic Shop is designed to be fun for magicians of all ages and abilities. Special attractions include live demonstrations and personal lessons on all tricks sold. The Houdini's Magic Shop branch at Caesar's Forum additionally houses a mini-museum that exhibits more than 100 of Houdini's tools and props, plus signed letters, shackles and photos. Geno's fascination with magic began as child but really took off after he broke his leg and discovered a book of magic. He later worked as a stage magician before opening the first Houdini's Magic Shop at the MGM Grand. Geno not only owns multiple magic stores—he even has an Italian restaurant and deli, Munari Produce at the Venetian. Explore the true magic of Las Vegas with a visit to any of the Houdini's Magic Shop locations.

6455 S Dean Martin Drive, Suite L, Las Vegas NV
(factory store and corporate headquarters)
(702) 798-4789 or (877) DINIWHO (346-4946)
www.houdini.com

Antiques at the Market

You might step through the doors of Antiques at the Market just as that doll that will complete your collection is arriving in the sales area. As collectors like to say, "You never know." With close to 100 vendors filling 24,000 square feet with their furniture, home accessories and collectibles, your odds of finding something you can't live without are extremely good at this Las Vegas market. What's more, you won't have to sift through a mess to find it. "We've been complimented that we're one of the cleanest antique shops around," says Liz Werner, who owns the business with her husband, Robert. Daughters Devon and Ryan are very active contributors. Everything from lamps and china to Indian artifacts and jewelry is contained under this one roof. Finds of Royal Doulton, Lalique and Tiffany are not uncommon. The merchandise quality is high, and it moves out the door quickly. "You're not going to see the same thing twice," says Liz. She says that the average customer spends about three hours taking it all in. Should hunger strike while you are browsing, you can take a break at the tearoom and café, where goodies are baked fresh daily. "The great thing is that you never know what you're going to see," says Liz, which, if you love antiques, is all you need to hear to get your pulse racing with anticipation. Feel the thrill of discovery with a visit to Antiques at the Market.

6665 S Eastern Avenue, Las Vegas NV
(702) 307-3960

Indra Grae Boutique

If you're looking for fun, trendy clothing and warm, personalized service, go directly to Indra Grae Boutique. Located in an unassuming strip mall, the boutique's warm teal walls and casual throw rugs evoke a comfortable feeling the moment you walk inside. Owner Mariah Lewis named the shop after her young daughter, and the boutique is as unique as its name. The shop features the work of several young up-and-coming designers. Mariah loves clothing from around the world, so the boutique's pieces have a fresh, multicultural feel. Sexy, old Hollywood styles offer comfortable, classically feminine looks with a hint of edginess, without the huge designer price tags. Indra Grae offers diversity in cuts, tailoring, shapes and fabrics to flatter each individual customer. The clothing comes in a range of sizes to fit real women. "The healthy look needs to come back," Mariah says. Friendly and helpful salespeople will help you put it all together, and the customer appreciation parties every few months are quite popular. Mariah's passion for fashion and background as a retail buyer prepared her for opening her own business in 2005. For a big city feel minus the stuffiness, come find your own look at Indra Grae Boutique.

6085 S Fort Apache Road, Suite 170, Las Vegas NV
(702) 636-9700

Victoria's Event Productions

Whether it's a corporate meeting or a convention attended by thousands of people, Victoria's Event Productions has the experience, skill and resources needed to make it an outstanding success. Victoria's Event Productions is a major player in the meeting and special event planning industry. "We bring ideas from a vision to reality, with attention to every detail," says owner Victoria Papageorge, who alone brings nearly 40 years of event production experience to her company. Along with her experience, Victoria brings all of her team's expertise together for each of her clients. In the past, companies would have to contact almost a dozen agencies to arrange their event. One call to Victoria's Event Productions does it all. Victoria and her staff design and create events, from stage design to lighting, unique talent, custom décor, flowers and linens. Victoria's Event Productions designs and manufactures props in-house. Additionally, Victoria's Event Productions is consistently seeking the most talented performers for business theater and corporate events. If you are planning an event, contact Victoria's Event Productions.

Las Vegas NV
(702) 794-2492 or (800) 317-7724
www.victoriasproductions.com

Ralph Jones Display

Family owned and operated for more than 40 years, Ralph Jones Display keeps Las Vegas decorated with convention displays, store fixtures and holiday decorating for both corporate and residential customers. The company not only designs, builds and installs fixtures, but can fabricate your own design concepts in its custom cabinet shop. Ralph Jones also maintains one of the largest year-round Christmas showrooms in the West and carries a complete assortment of bows, ribbons, garlands and ornaments of every color and style. The company specializes in oversized wreaths. Decorator trees come in a variety of styles from two to 25 feet in height for interior application. Custom trees for outdoor use that are up to 100 feet tall. If you're unsure of the look you want, talented designers here will help you choose from a multitude of themes and take your decorating ideas from concept to reality. Not just a resource for Christmas, Ralph Jones Display can craft seasonal displays for any holiday from Easter to Halloween and will ship anywhere in the world. The company has the ability to create the special effects you desire, from banners to animation. Ralph Jones Display will design, fabricate, install and take down all seasonal displays. This is the company that decorates for the Las Vegas stars and creates the displays along the Las Vegas strip. Bring some of that glitter to your home and office with a visit to Ralph Jones Display.

2576 E Charleston Boulevard, Las Vegas NV
(702) 382-4398
www.ralphjones.com

Executive Floral Design Services

When extraordinary floral design is what you need, Executive Floral Design Services has the answer. Executive Floral offers a full line of services, from weddings to welcome gifts and everything in between. Mike Sinanovic is the creative force that drives Executive Floral. His original designs include many striking arrangements featuring orchids. Sinanovic's elegant Ikabana is an award-winning design that depicts three levels of life—Heaven, Man and Earth. Networking with fellow professionals makes it possible for Executive Floral to accommodate all facets of event planning, down to entertainment and transportation. Sinanovic, who unlike most florists is certified by the American Institute of Floral Designers, brought 30 years of floral design experience with him when he moved to Las Vegas. Educated in the United States and the Netherlands, Sinanovic also spent time as a floral designer in Malaysia. Sinanovic's design history is impressive. He was a chosen florist for the American visit of Pope John Paul II, a featured designer on the Rose Bowl float and an invited guest designer for a Presidential inaugural. Try Executive Floral Design Services for a theme party or birthday bash, and prepare to be awed.

3111 S Valley View Boulevard, Suite J-101, Las Vegas NV
(702) 633-5024
www.executivefloral.com

Wild Truffles Catering

Wild Truffles Catering, voted the Best Caterer in Las Vegas by *Las Vegas Life Magazine*, can turn your next event or business function into a memorable occasion. Whether you are planning an executive deli lunch, cocktail party or something more elaborate, this caterer is your gourmet restaurant on the go, bringing a wealth of expertise to your affair. Owners Eva and Georg Paulussen add an international influence to their menus, thanks to their background and experience. Eva was born in Jamaica and Georg in Germany. They have worked in New York, New Jersey, Boston, London, Germany, Japan, India and the Bahamas. As the executive chef, Georg focuses on taste, texture and presentation, a trio that promises that your guest will be entertained while enjoying tasty and attractive food choices. Georg, Eva and their experienced staff have a combined 100 years of culinary experience. Their menu and event coordination are personalized to meet your needs. To entertain your guests and provide high-quality gourmet options, the Wild Truffles staff begins by creating a serviceable kitchen at your venue. Wild Truffles Catering not only takes care of the food, they can organize all the flowers, tables, chairs, linens and tents. They even provide such luxuries as ice carvings and decorations for themed events. These special event wizards will be ready for your guests with china, stemware and flatware. Steel drummers, a disk jockey, valet parking, photography and videography are other services that can be arranged. Whether you want a sit-down multi-course meal or live action station buffet in your home or on the range, turn to Wild Truffles Catering for excellence.

7905 W Sahara Avenue, Suite #106, Las Vegas NV (702) 242-1542 *www.wild-truffles.com*

Emerald at Queensridge

Planning an important party can be quite the challenge if you don't have the correct tools—such as the telephone number for Emerald at Queensridge. This gracious five-star property is a full service single-event facility that specializes in customer service and attentive attention to the fine details. The elegant venue is neither a country club nor a hotel yet it offers all of the luxurious amenities one would expect in either. Emerald at Queensridge features a lush outdoor garden, an ideal backdrop for weddings, along with a grand staircase and an elegant dining room. Spacious bride and groom suites are outfitted with everything from makeup mirrors for the ladies to golf putting green for the gents. The exquisitely designed premises are ideal for holiday parties, award banquets and luncheons, as well as weddings or fundraisers of nearly any size. Owners Renae and Leon Iunco began their career photographing special events. They were able to fulfill a long held dream of owning their own banquet facility when they purchased Emerald at Queensridge (formerly Emerald Gardens) in 2006. Ensure that your grand event is a stunning success with a simple call to the caring professionals of Emerald at Queensridge.

891 S Rampart Boulevard, Las Vegas NV
(702) 242-5700
www.emeraldatqueensridge.com

A Special Memory Wedding Chapel

All wedding packages at A Special Memory Wedding Chapel include complimentary limousine service. This means that you can enjoy the best of two worlds—a ride in luxury combined with a ceremony at a quaint, old-fashioned chapel that would not look out of place in a historic New England village. Actually, you can choose from two chapels: the main A Special Memory with seating for up to 100 and the smaller Royal Chapel that seats about 35. Stained glass, an organ and rich romantic colors make either a perfect setting for your ceremony. Owner Gordon Gust, who has been facilitating weddings since 1973, knows the business. His packages cover every last detail, even including the services of a wedding coordinator. This person will advise you on how to line up to go down the aisle and will give the bride directions for making her grand entrance from the top of the stairs into the chapel. If you prefer an outdoor wedding at a breathtaking location, Gordon provides Weddings to Go at Red Rock Canyon or Valley of Fire. He arranges ceremonies in hot-air balloons, in helicopters and on horseback. His wedding themes include NASCAR, Harley Davidson and Star Trek. For a quaint ceremony or a myriad of other options, consider A Special Memory Wedding Chapel.

800 S 4th Street, Las Vegas NV
(702) 384-2211 or (800) 962-7798

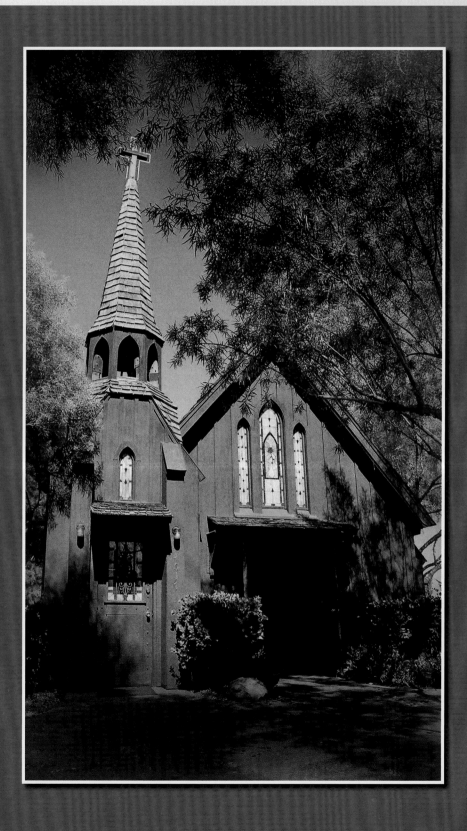

The Little Church of the West

In a town known for its dazzling modern buildings, couples are drawn to the Little Church of the West, a wedding chapel on the Las Vegas Strip, because of its unique facade. Built in 1942 as part of the Last Frontier Hotel resort, Little Church of the West is a replica of a Western mining town church. From its hanging Victorian lamps to its pipe organ, the chapel captures the quaint charm of the 19th century. The exterior is made completely from cedar; the interior is made from stained and varnished California redwood. The Little Church of the West has been moved twice over the years, but at no time has the building been used for anything other than performing marriage ceremonies. It was the first structure to be built in Las Vegas specifically for that use. Because of its distinctive architecture and its significant contribution to Nevada's cultural history, the church is listed on the National Register of Historic Places, making it the only place on the Strip with this designation. Richard Gere and Cindy Crawford were married here as were Billy Bob Thornton and Angelina Jolie. Celebrity weddings from earlier days include those of Judy Garland, Mickey Rooney and Red Foxx. If you are considering a wedding in Las Vegas, drop by the Little Church of the West, and fall in love with its simple beauty and sentimental history.

4617 Las Vegas Boulevard S, Las Vegas NV
(702) 739-7971 or (800) 821-2452
www.littlechurchlv.com

Graceland Wedding Chapel

Brendan Paul as Elvis

For the same price as a standard wedding package at the Graceland Wedding Chapel, you could have Elvis give the bride away and sing two songs, one before and one after the ceremony. Co-owner of the chapel, Brendan Duffy, has made his living as an Elvis impersonator. He is, in fact, the impersonator of choice for many venues in Las Vegas. Most of all, he loves to melt hearts when he serenades couples at his Graceland chapel. Other Elvis packages are available, including the Concert with the King, which features Elvis performing five songs—one before, one during and three after the ceremony. Do you want the supreme Elvis experience? That would be the Famous Dueling Elvis Package in which two different Elvis impersonators participate in the ceremony, one a young buck in gold lamé; the other, a 1970s Las Vegas Elvis in a jumpsuit. All packages, whether traditional or with Elvis, include flowers and photography. Originally built as a house in the 1920s, the Graceland Wedding Chapel is located on the Strip, although from inside you will feel miles away from the hustle and bustle just outside the door. To book your Elvis wedding, contact the Graceland Wedding Chapel today.

619 Las Vegas Boulevard, Las Vegas NV
(702) 382-0091 or (800) 824-5732
www.gracelandchapel.com

Viva Las Vegas Wedding Chapel

Are you dreaming of a fantasy-filled themed wedding? Perhaps you've always wanted a romantic traditional wedding with all the trimmings. Whatever you envision as the perfect wedding, Viva Las Vegas Wedding Chapel will make it come alive. Owner Ron Decar has been in the wedding business for 10 years and offers the attention to detail and outstanding customer service that will make your special day a memorable occasion. Formerly a singer at the Tropicana, Ron was often asked to dress as Elvis when he moonlighted as a singer at weddings. Since opening the chapel, Ron has expanded his repertoire of wedding themes, and today Viva Las Vegas specializes in 25 imaginative scenarios, complete with fog and theatrical lighting, including Elvis, Blue Hawaii, Camelot, Gothic, Gangster, Fairytale, Egyptian and Pirate. The chapel offers celebrity impersonator ceremonies with Tom Jones, Marilyn, Sinatra, Bond and Austin, Baby. Viva Las Vegas also organizes scenic helicopter weddings in the Grand Canyon. The chapel broadcasts over the Internet, so your family and friends can see and hear your wedding free of charge. Chapel employees all have entertainment backgrounds, so expect professional performances. *Nevada Magazine* readers voted the chapel the Best Las Vegas Wedding Chapel for six years in a row. Whether you desire a quiet outdoor ceremony in a vine-covered gazebo or want to roll down the aisle with Elvis in a real pink Caddy, let Viva Las Vegas Wedding Chapel make your wedding day dreams come true.

1205 Las Vegas Boulevard S, Las Vegas NV
(702) 384-0771 of (800) 574-4450 *www.vivalasvegas.com*

Get Lei'd

Travelers from around the world know they can experience the spirit of *aloha* on the Hawaiian Islands, where giving a lei is a symbol of love and friendship. In Las Vegas, the Hawaiian custom is alive and well at Get Lei'd, a local flower shop created by Willie Salavera. Willie has supplied his flower leis for events at Margaritaville and the MGM Grand, as well as for concerts by Kelly Clarkson, Brad Paisley and Jimmy Buffet. The shop's fresh Pacific island flower leis are popular at weddings and graduations. The styles and plant materials vary. Consider a single or double lei made of Dendrobium orchids or revel in the heady scent of tuberose, alone or combined with orchids. Braided leaves of the green ti plant dry well, and the double yellow plumeria offers light fragrance and sunny color. The EleEle Crimson Thai Orchid lei is particularly festive, with more than 1,000 dark orchid petals positioned with meticulous precision. Leis can be hand delivered in Las Vegas or shipped overnight to other cities. Many stay fresh up to 10 days with proper care. They can also be dried to preserve memories of a special event for years to come. If you are designing a sandal-clad wedding or a Polynesian-themed occasion, ask about discounts on an order of 10 or more leis. For the feel of warm tropical breezes and sand under your feet, order an exotic flower necklace from Get Lei'd.

3988 Tirana Way, Las Vegas NV
(702) 366-1800
www.getleidinc.com

Couture Bride

The three fashion industry veterans who opened Couture Bride in December 2006 intended to set a new standard for bridal salons in the Las Vegas area. The selection of gowns alone puts this shop in a class of its own. Couture Bride is the exclusive Nevada retailer of designer gowns by Vera Wang, Carolina Herrera, Oscar de la Renta and Monique Lhuillier as well as Elizabeth Fillmore, Ulla Maija and the Platinum Collection. The salon's complete inventory includes bridesmaids' gowns, too, along with veils and headpieces. Co-owners Dawn Heaney and Flora Petakas Marinelli learned luxury while working as executives for Vera Wang in New York City. The third partner, Annette Cirillo-Bergen, worked for various Italian silk mills before opening fashion showrooms in Manhattan. Las Vegas lacked a full-service luxury bridal salon until this dynamic trio joined forces. "Every detail of Couture Bride encompasses luxury and chic sophistication," says Annette. "The shop is modern, sophisticated and elegant," Dawn agrees, adding that customers should not feel intimidated by designer gowns. "Selecting your bridal gown will be a uniquely warm and inviting experience within the especially romantic yet exciting environment we have created," she says. Find the standard for bridal sophistication at Couture Bride.

950 S Durango Drive, Suite 130, Las Vegas NV
(702) 647-7778
www.couturebridelv.com

HalloweenMart

HalloweenMart launched its website in 1994 and quickly emerged as a leading provider of costumes and decorations for Halloween. Starting out as a small family owned and operated business, it wasn't long before the Siegel family was selling costumes year-round from its retail store and website, which earned the *Wall Street Journal's* Best of the Web award. Their 20,000-square-foot headquarters and showroom is just five minutes from the Las Vegas strip, giving residents a year-round opportunity to prepare for parties and events. With costumes and accessories for all sizes, HalloweenMart can transform you into a specific movie character, a historical figure or a scary monster. Superheroes, cartoon characters and adorable animal outfits delight children, from infants to teens. Costumes for the holidays, school plays and theatrical productions are always in demand. You can even dress your dog in a top hat and tails or a Batman suit. If you need to *haunt* your house, HalloweenMart has hundreds of life-size props, lights and decorations to help you create that ghoulish graveyard, spooky scene or party atmosphere. Whether you come into a retail store or buy online, you're sure to be pleased with over 10,000 costumes and decorations at your disposal. No matter what the season or reason, come to HalloweenMart and let them dress you up.

www.HalloweenMart.com

Weddings by Classical Entertainment, Inc.

Classical Entertainment offers upscale music for weddings and other special events in the Las Vegas Valley or the destination of your choice. These wedding services cater to the discerning bride whose high expectations draw her to the finest professionals, capable of gracing her event with sparkling bravura. Whether it is a large wedding or a small, intimate group, a second-time-around celebration or a vow renewal, Classical Entertainment can supply the ambience to make your wedding dreams come true. Classical Entertainment can provide music for both the ceremony and the reception. Ceremonial music may include familiar classics that announce the entrance of the bride's mother, the bride and the groom, as well as selections that have special meaning to the bridal couple. Processional and recessional trumpets add a dramatic touch, and vocalists are available for special selections. Several options are available for the reception, depending upon your style, flair and taste. For the smaller, intimate gathering a jazz trio or signature pop fusion group can add a delightful backdrop for guests who want to converse. For a larger, party-oriented occasion, the firm can supply the finest dance bands and high energy DJ's. For your special day, contact Classical Entertainment for music that will make your event more than memorable.

7380 S Eastern Avenue, Suite 124-307, Las Vegas NV
(702) 558-2973
www.classicalentertainment.com

Best Wedding Favors

When Pat Custer first came to Las Vegas from Thailand to attend the University of Nevada, she never expected to meet her future husband, Charles, and make the city her home, but that is exactly what happened. Today, Pat and Charles are the proud owners of Best Wedding Favors, a company specializing in personalized favors. Wedding guests in Thailand are honored with small gifts from the happy couple, a custom that is also honored at many American weddings. The Custers noticed that shops specializing in small gifts were scarce in Las Vegas and started Best Wedding Favors as an online company in 2000, and expended their operation to include a storefront in the upscale suburb of Henderson. Best Wedding Favors offers a huge selection of clever favors, most priced under two dollars. The shop can customize and personalize nearly anything, including invitations, playing cards, poker chips with your photo and shot glasses. In additional to wedding favors and such supplies as wedding cake toppers, guest book and pen sets, ring pillows and flower girl baskets, the shop stocks favors for such special occasions as anniversaries, baby showers, graduations, birthdays and house warming parties. Best Wedding Favors also offers onsite engraving. You can purchase everything you need to make a goodie bag or let Pat and her staff assemble custom selections for you. Ensure that no guest leaves empty handed with favors and gifts from Best Wedding Favors.

213 N Stephanie Street, Suite G, Henderson NV
(702) 436-9955 *www.bestweddingfavors.com*

All About You Bridal Galleria

When it comes to weddings, it's all about the bride, and when it comes to the bride, finding the perfect gown is a priority. All About You Bridal Galleria in Las Vegas showcases an extraordinary selection of exquisite bridal gowns, with many exclusive lines, such as Pronovias, Justine McCaffrey and Sposa by St. Pucchi. Co-owners Laura Strade and daughters Kari Peltier and Tara Jones offer much more than a bridal boutique. They go the extra mile to provide complete wedding planning services. Customers can relax over a cup of tea in the elegant library while pouring over catalogs devoted to gowns, floral arrangements, invitations, photography, cakes and gifts. The shop also screens vendors to get the best prices and services and can provide referrals for reception and honeymoon plans as well as rehearsal dinners. The owners maintain relationships with their brides, who often come back to update them on married life after the wedding. Laura has even given out her home phone number to reassure nervous brides and has rescued brides at the last minute who couldn't figure out how to put on a bustle or a gown on the day of the wedding. From tuxedos and bridesmaids' apparel to referrals and advice on etiquette, All About You is all about the perfect wedding day. Start you wedding plans with professional services from All About You Bridal Galleria.

2470 E Pebble Road, Suite 114, Henderson NV
(702) 269-9333
www.allaboutyoubridalgalleria.com

Charolette Richards–
Little White Wedding Chapel

Charolette Richards has been in the marriage business for over 48 years and has helped the Little White Wedding Chapel become one of the most popular places to tie the knot. Hundreds of thousands of couples have been married at the Little White Wedding Chapel and Charolette is hoping to celebrate the millionth couple by the year 2010. Charolette has been a trendsetter in the wedding industry with such original weddings as the first hot air balloon wedding and the original Drive Thru Tunnel of Vows, which has become popular for thousands of couples, such as bikers, roller skaters and even some who walk through. Charolette was also the first to offer free limo service. She is the creator of the Elvis-themed wedding that uses a pink Cadillac convertible, called A Tribute to Elvis, and was actually a part of Elvis and Priscilla's wedding. Charolette was the first to create helicopter weddings, and has married couples on roller coasters, boats, aircraft, waterslides and underwater. She officiated the first televised wedding on *Live with Regis and Kathie Lee* and pioneered live Internet weddings. Little White Wedding Chapel may sound small, but the amenities say otherwise. It has five chapels on the property, a limousine service, on-site tux and gown rentals plus alterations, floral and photography services and a web cam. Celebrities married here include Frank Sinatra, Michael Jordan, Bruce Willis, Joan Collins and many others. "I love to make people happy. I pray for all couples and tell them not to look at their faults but to look at the good," Charolette says. "We call all our couples stars, because that's what they really are."

1301 Las Vegas Boulevard S, Las Vegas NV
(702) 382-5943 or (800) 545-8111
www.alittlewhitechapel.com

Photo by Burton Lo

Pump It Up

When folks in southern Nevada want jumping entertainment for the whole family, they turn to Pump It Up. Doug Laudenslager opened the innovative franchise in 2004 to provide families an exciting alternative to the standard youth party venues. This huge indoor facility, with locations in both Las Vegas and Henderson, offers inflatable play structures for staging birthday parties, scout troop events or other group gatherings. Even if you don't have an event to celebrate, you can bring the kids for Pop In Playtime on weekday mornings. Adults can play right along with kids in a variety of inventive structures. With a 12,000-square-foot building designed for clean, safe fun and private party rooms that comfortably accommodate large groups, celebrating a special event at Pump It Up couldn't be easier. The staff provides assistance with all aspects of your planned party, whether large or small, including optional pizza and soda packages, goodie bags and balloons. Cleanup is included, which is music to any exhausted parents' ears. Kids and adults alike love the lively atmosphere. If your kids are climbing the walls and you've got a sense of adventure, bring some socks and visit Pump It Up. It'll put the bounce back in your step.

3200 W. Sunset Road, Suite 100, Las Vegas NV
(702) 568-5204
7685 Commercial Way, Suite G/H, Henderson NV
(702) 568-5204
www.pumpitupparty.com

Executive Floral Design Services

When extraordinary floral design is what you need, Executive Floral Design Services has the answer. Executive Floral offers a full line of services, from weddings to welcome gifts and everything in between. Mike Sinanovic is the creative force that drives Executive Floral. His original designs include many striking arrangements featuring orchids. Sinanovic's elegant Ikabana is an award-winning design that depicts three levels of life—Heaven, Man and Earth. Networking with fellow professionals makes it possible for Executive Floral to accommodate all facets of event planning, down to entertainment and transportation. Sinanovic, who unlike most florists is certified by the American Institute of Floral Designers, brought 30 years of floral design experience with him when he moved to Las Vegas. Educated in the United States and the Netherlands, Sinanovic also spent time as a floral designer in Malaysia. Sinanovic's design history is impressive. He was a chosen florist for the American visit of Pope John Paul II, a featured designer on the Rose Bowl float and an invited guest designer for a Presidential inaugural. Try Executive Floral Design Services for a theme party or birthday bash, and prepare to be awed.

3111 S Valley View Boulevard, Suite J-101, Las Vegas NV
(702) 633-5024
www.executivefloral.com

The Ivy House & Garden Florist

With so many things to think about as your wedding day approaches, it's comforting to know that the Ivy House & Garden Florist is taking care of the flowers. Jamie Zaleski and her staff have a reputation for exceptional service, no matter what the size of your wedding. They will work within your budget to create a look that expresses the love and joy of that day. If you would prefer a custom design, Jamie and her staff can create a work of floral elegance for everything from the altar arrangement at the ceremony to the centerpieces at the reception. They even have ideas for the garland around your guest book. Jamie and her staff are ready to apply the same creativity to any special event that you may be planning, from family reunions to business luncheons. Are you thinking of a contemporary design, traditional, eclectic or some unique in-between blend? They will listen to your needs and show you the possibilities for a personalized design. For exquisite floral arrangements to express your sentiments, come to the Ivy House & Garden Florist. You are also invited to visit the Ivy House website for more information or to order online.

**9340 W Sahara Avenue,
Suite 100, Las Vegas NV
(702) 360-0800**
www.ivyflowerslv.com

Amazing Clowns

Husband and wife team Ray and Christine Wold cater to both the young and the young at heart through their comic company Amazing Clowns. This dynamic pair came to Nevada to perform in Cirque du Soleil's O at the Bellagio. Looking for a performance-based side business, they happened upon the idea of doing birthday parties. Ray, formerly a clown with Ringling Brothers, put his experience to good use. He quickly gained a word-of-mouth reputation for putting on a terrific show in a town known for its entertainment. Amazing Clowns specializes in creating happy memories that will last a lifetime. Amazing Clowns can bring a clown, princess, pirate, magician, disk jockey or a variety of other entertainers to your location. Alternatively, have a fun and fabulous party at Amazing Clowns' 5,100-square-foot indoor facility. The Amazing Clowns party park offers a two-hour special with free video games at the in-house arcade, free pizza, popcorn and cotton candy and balloons, along with a clown show and a dance contest with prizes. The center also rents out bouncy castles, carnival games, cotton candy machines, trains, Ferris wheels and much more. There's a spiffy magic shop and a great catering department fulfills your one-stop party needs. Delight your child and the child within by scheduling Amazing Clowns for your next party.

3525 E Flamingo Road, Las Vegas NV
(702) 434-6222
www.amazingclowns.com

Kathy Kavanaugh, The Singing Harpist

Kathy Kavanaugh has a beautiful 23-karat golden harp and sings in seven different languages: English, French, Spanish, Italian, Tagalog, Hebrew and German. She also plays piano. Kathy is available for many types of occasions, from weddings, birthdays, corporate events, memorials, art shows, teas or concerts. She is also a harp therapist. For centuries, music has shared an important relationship with the body and its healing properties. Kathy brings a resonance of well-being and health to her clients through her exquisite and soothing harp music. Although Kathy did not take up the harp until she was in her 30s, she imparts an ease and warmth to her music that comes with experience and an astounding natural talent. Kathy was recently featured on NBC's *America's Got Talent*, sang at book signings for Deepak Chopra, and has performed for former President Jimmy Carter and motivational speaker Tony Robbins. She is a firm believer in harp and sound therapy and gives private or group sessions that include breathing, visualization, and relaxation exercises to slow your heart rate and create harmony and balance in your body. Kathy can customize your session to fit your individual needs. She encourages her clients to experience the true relaxation and healing that harp music can bring to all who listen. Kathy has two CDs available, *Love Songs* and *Lift Your Spirits*, and she is producing a DVD of her music. Call Kathy Kavanaugh today and bring peace and harmony back into your life.

Las Vegas NV (702) 340-3030
Oceanside CA (760) 889-3340
www.singingharpist.com www.harpnosis.com

The Victoria's Family

You are assured a wedding day filled with magical moments, thanks to the elite services of The Victoria's Family, Las Vegas' premier collection of wedding venues. The Victoria's Family founded itself in 1990, over the years this unique family has gained a stellar reputation for their exquisite weddings and receptions. The Victoria's Family features three distinct venues for your nuptials. The newly designed Victoria's Chapel contains solid oak pews, fine embroidery and a sky mural on the ceiling, while the Embassy Terrace offers the grandeur of cathedral ceilings and crystal chandeliers. El Caribe, with its soaring palms, brings classic charm to intimate or large celebrations of up to 300 guests. The Victoria's Family provides professional photographers who utilize an in-house photo lab and world-class cuisine prepared to order by the company's own caterers. Victoria's also offers custom wedding cakes and floral arrangements, chauffeured limousines, and DJ services that help to ensure your celebration is perfect down to the last detail. The staff at The Victoria's Family are dedicated to taking the stress out of planning a wedding and offer a selection of specialized, all-inclusive, packages that will allow you to easily customize your wedding day with no hidden expenses or unexpected surprises. Whether you're planning a wedding, corporate meeting, or other special event, celebrate your big day in style and elegance with a little help from the experts at The Victoria's Family.

2800 W Sahara Avenue, Las Vegas NV
(702) 252-4565 or (800) 344-5683
www.victoriasfamily.com

Lakeside Weddings and Events

Inside the gates at Lakeside Weddings and Events, you know you are in a better place. The events facility is located on the outskirts of Summerlin on the shores of Lake Jacqueline. "You feel like you aren't in Las Vegas, but in a beautiful, pastoral, intimate area," says General Manager Melissa Arechiga. "Unforgettable … That's what we are." Everyone who works at Lakeside Weddings seeks to make your visit here unforgettable, from the chefs and servers to the groundskeepers and the staff at the on- site spa and salon. The events specialist here is adept at arranging for all aspects of your wedding or conference in a facility that can comfortably handle up to 200 guests. During the week, Lakeside provides catering and audiovisual equipment for corporate meetings, while weekends are devoted to weddings. With the help of the Lakeside staff, even the most elaborate wedding becomes manageable. You can choose a lakeside ceremony and a full floral package with the knowledge that Lakeside's on-site coordinator has thought of everything from the wedding official of your choice to your rehearsal needs. Lakeside offers a choice of catering services, from hors d'oeuvre receptions and buffets to hosted bars and sit-down dinners featuring Lakeside's notable French cuisine. Lakeside can arrange for photography, a wedding cake, an emcee or disc jockey and limo service to whisk the bride and groom away at the close of the reception. For attention to detail and fairytale surroundings you will remember always, plan your wedding or special event at Lakeside Weddings and Events.

2620 Regatta Drive, Suite 102, Las Vegas NV
(702) 240-5290
www.lakesideweddings.com

CLM Weddings

Love may be complicated, but it's often a lot simpler than coordinating the wedding. That's where CLM Weddings comes in. Once you have hired this company as your wedding consultant, you will enjoy unlimited pre-planning hours as well as unlimited wedding day hours. CLM Weddings works one-on-one with clients to design a look for the wedding, select the venue and vendors and manage budgeting and timelines. "I want couples to look back and say they enjoyed their weddings," says owner Christie McCoy, whose motto is Your Day Your Way. She describes herself as a hopeless romantic who has always loved weddings. Her flair for design became obvious at a young age. "I was the child who re-arranged her bedroom because she loved the concept of design," she says. Working for companies that coordinated corporate events prepared her for starting her own business. Christie and her crew will be there for you after the wedding, too, returning tuxes to their rental shop. They'll even take care of your pet while you are on your honeymoon. Perhaps the best wedding gift you can give yourself is the knowledge that everything is under control as your big day approaches. Gain the freedom to enjoy your wedding by leaving the complications to CLM Weddings.

Las Vegas NV
(702) 982-2129
www.clmweddings.com

Something Blue

Something Blue features couture bridal gowns and bridesmaid dresses in a variety of styles from lacey traditional to strapless chic. Something Blue is the exclusive Vegas-area source for stunning gowns from top designers such as Rivini, Anne Barge, Alvina Valenta, Jenny Lee and Henry Roth. The boutique offers two bride's lounges where the bride and her family and friends can relax in a comfortable private setting while they share the experience of choosing the bride's gown and the wedding party attire. Experienced bridal consultants assist the bridal party in selecting the veil, shoes, headpieces and accessories. Something Blue is associated with professional floral designers who can provide all custom floral needs, and it can recommend like-minded vendors such as photographers and invitation printers. Anna Wilson Perez opened her bridal boutique in February 2006 after gaining years of experience in the hotel and floral design industries. Anna's goal is to provide an alternative to impersonal warehouse-style bridal stores. "I want customers to feel that Something Blue exceeds their expectations," she explains. "I want them to feel like they're dealing with a friend, not just a salesperson." For exquisite gown selection and personalized attention that will make you feel special on your special day, come to Something Blue.

6345 S Rainbow Boulevard, Suite 102, Las Vegas NV
(702) 243-2226
www.somethingbluelv.com

International Wine Cellar & Havana Cigar Bar

Many people feel there's nothing more relaxing than an outstanding glass of wine and a first-rate cigar. If this describes you, your first stop in Las Vegas should be the International Wine Cellar & Havana Cigar Bar. In the process of creating their own special world, proprietors Johnny and Eileen Devito have fashioned a charming hideaway with a European flair right here in Las Vegas. The establishment is open from 9 am to midnight daily, and patrons can enjoy fine wine, smooth cigars or both in a relaxing atmosphere with live entertainment three nights a week. Wine connoisseurs can enjoy domestic wines as well as international ones, and for those who can't tell the difference, wine classes are available, instructed by knowledgeable sommeliers. Cigar aficionados can indulge in hand-rolled cigars of the finest quality from such exotic locales as the Dominican Republic, Honduras and Nicaragua. You can also choose a hand-rolled treasure from the Havana Cigar Bar's master roller. If you are planning a private function, such as a corporate event or bachelor party, you can book the cigar bar and benefit from the services of a helpful staff, who are eager to assist you every step of the way. Break out of your old routine with a visit to the International Wine Cellar & Havana Cigar Bar and watch your troubles go up in smoke.

3900 Paradise Road, Las Vegas NV
(702) 892-9555 or (800) 866-6748
www.havanasmoke.com

Khoury's Fine Wine & Spirits

"Wine doesn't have to be a snobby thing," says Issa Khoury, who co-owns Khoury's Fine Wine & Spirits with his wife, Nura. The Khourys pride themselves on the casual atmosphere of their Henderson store, which opened in 2004, and their Las Vegas store, which opened in 2006. Khoury's is a place where wine lovers and novices both enjoy congregating to experience new flavors. "We want to make it non-intimidating to people," Issa says. The store stocks boutique wines—as many as 2,000 different brands. Among the rare wines are those offered by Palm Cellars, which produces a limited 545 cases per year. The store also stocks wines from other countries, such as Italy, France, Spain, Portugal and Lebanon. You also will find American microbrewed beers and fine cognac, single malt scotch and tequila. The store is very customer-oriented. If what you want is not in stock, Khoury's can special order it. Khoury's offers weekly wine tastings to educate customers. Issa has completed classes through the International Sommelier Guild to learn about the intricacies of wine. For a store that's Big Enough to Serve and Small Enough to Care, come to Khoury's Fine Wine & Spirits.

9915 S Eastern Avenue, Suite 110, Henderson NV
(702) 435-9463
7150 S Durango Drive, Suite 110, Las Vegas NV
(702) 453-9463
www.khourysfinewine.com

Hot air balloons lighting up the Reno night sky

Reno Area

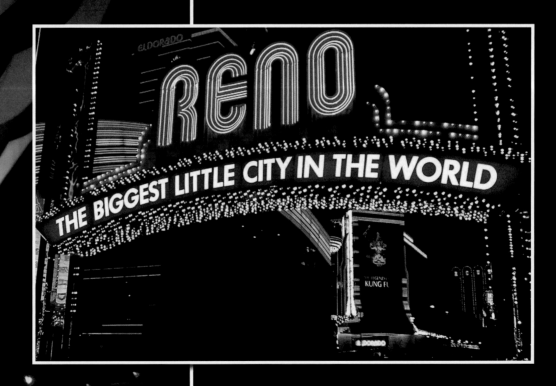

Kids & Horses
Therapeutic Riding Center

A disability may leave a child unable to walk, but that doesn't mean the kid can't gallop. Founded in 1999, Kids & Horses is a program that offers horsemanship as a means to improve strength, balance, coordination and self-esteem. In spite of blindness, cerebral palsy, Down's syndrome and other disabilities, many students go on to own and care for their own horses. "It can be done," says Curt Wegener, finance director of Kids & Horses. "All it takes is an interest in horses and a willingness to stretch body, mind and spirit." Certified instructors provide individually tailored riding lessons. While the name Kids & Horses implies that the program works solely with children, about 20 per cent of the students are adults. All services are provided at a modest cost to participants. Businesses, organizations and individuals support the program through contributions and donations of equipment. Indeed, the way that the community has responded to the program's needs is heartwarming. The Reno Rodeo Association recently provided a three-horse trailer so that Kids & Horses can take children to competitions all over the Western states. Perhaps you can lend your support by giving a saddle or some water buckets. Contact Kids & Horses to make a donation or to discover how the program can inspire someone you know to overcome a disability.

2869 Esaw Street, Minden NV
(775) 267-1775
www.kidsandhorses.org

Reno Retreats LLC

Reno Retreats offers a welcome alternative to motels and hotels. Lisa and John offer fully furnished and landscaped homes that Reno-area visitors can rent for stays of two days or longer. Especially suitable for groups traveling together or families with children or pets, the homes also work well for Reno residents who need lodging for out-of-town guests. Each southwest Reno home is just minutes from the nightlife and special events downtown, skiing at Lake Tahoe, and the area's many local golf courses, yet far enough away to provide a quiet and private retreat for guests and their families or friends. Home sizes range from the 850-square-foot Virginia Lake Condo to Mt. Rose, a 3,300-square-foot home with five bedrooms, four baths, a pool table and sauna. Visitors bringing valuable possessions such as expensive motorcycles or antique cars to special events in Reno will appreciate the one or two-car lockable garages in all homes except the condo. Every home features televisions with DVDs and VCRs, local telephone service and a fireplace. You'll find cooking your own meals is a pleasure in beautifully appointed kitchens complete with microwaves, dishwashers and all cookware, dishes and utensils. The homes are smoke-free, but smokers can relax on the patios. Whether you need a cottage for two or accommodations for your entire extended family, book your next Nevada getaway at Reno Retreats. You'll agree there's no place like home.

**550 W Plumb Lane, Suite B-272, Reno NV
(775) 745-2818**
www.renoretreats.com

Silverland USA Ramada

Visitors arriving in the Comstock-era mining town of Virginia City will find a new hotel on the scene, the community's first multi-million dollar inn. With architecture that fits the standards of Virginia City's historical district, the sparkling Silverland USA Ramada offers 68 comfortable guest rooms, a restaurant, salon, meeting rooms and casino. The first of its three floors overlooks the Comstock Park Arena, site of the annual camel races that are the town's most popular tourist event. Owner Hugh Roy Marshall calls the Silverland USA Ramada his railroad hotel, because it stands along the route of the Virginia & Truckee Railroad. Marshall owns quite a bit of Virginia City, it seems, including a downtown shop called the Marshall Mint. Drop by and check out the selection of silver and jewelry. Marshall hopes to return Virginia City to its silver-plated glory by excavating two mining shafts, one of which will be developed as an interactive tourist attraction. He also is considering plans to construct more hotels, a theme park and an underground roller coaster. Tourism officials see the Silverland USA Ramada as a harbinger of a new era for Virginia City. If everything goes according to plan, the town will soon offer an array of tourist attractions to go along with its appeal as a shop-lined historic district. Expect a most pleasant stay in Virginia City when you choose the Silverland USA Ramada.

146 South D Street, Virginia City NV
(775) 847-0571

Comstock Park

For more than a decade, Comstock Park has been a center of social activity and tourism in Virginia City, hosting a range of community events in its public recreation arena. The park is now the site of a major real estate development that will include a Ramada Inn, the Wild Rose Restaurant and the Silverland Saloon and Casino. Hugh Marshall, the owner of Comstock Park Company, is building on the historic site of the Comstock Lode, America's first major silver ore deposit. Discovered in 1859, the Comstock Lode is Virginia City's claim to fame, the source of its wealth and the origin of its tourist industry. Dan DeQuille's 1874 book, *A History of the Big Bonanza,* immortalized the site. In letters to DeQuille, Mark Twain coined the name Silverland to describe Virginia City. Marshall recognized the importance of the city's rich history in naming his enterprises, the first tourist businesses in the Comstock Lode area. In the last decade, Comstock Park has seen a new influx of tourists attending the annual Virginia City Camel Races. A Virginia City tradition since 1960, the races have been international competitions since 1987 and attract thousands of visitors every year. Comstock Park's current plans include an expansion of its outdoor arena to accommodate rodeos and horse shows in addition to races and fairs. Visit Comstock Park to explore the historic Lode, attend Virginia City events, and enjoy the city's first family resort destination.

**146 South D Street, Virginia City NV
(775) 847-0571**

Genoa Lakes Golf Club and Resort

Two championship courses just two miles apart await golfers at Genoa Lakes Golf Club and Resort. The eastern slopes of the breathtaking Sierra Nevada Mountains are the setting. The challenges at both courses are, in a word, tough. You'll need power and distance at the Resort Course. More than 100 bunkers, unpredictable mountain terrain, afternoon breezes and a waterfall challenge are some of the perils you'll encounter. At the Lakes Course, lush wetlands and the winding Carson River bring water into 14 holes of play. Hit your drives long and keep them straight, or you may have a splash landing. If the going is rough, you can always take solace in the wide-open spaces and spectacular high desert scenery. If you hold your own against either of these two courses, you'll be smiling for hours, perhaps even days. The clubhouse at the Lakes Course offers a European-style atmosphere and serves everything from snacks at the Sports Club to elegant, fireside Italian dining at Antoci's. The mood is more rustic at the Resort Club clubhouse, where the Alpine Room serves lunch and dinner. Try the snack bar for a quick bite. For banquets, weddings and meetings, both clubhouses include spacious rooms with views. Bring your best game to Genoa Lakes Golf Club and Resort.

1 Genoa Lakes Drive, Genoa NV (775) 782-4653
www.genoalakes.com

Carson Valley Inn

In 1983, Patrick and Jeane Mulreany had the idea of opening a small restaurant. This notion soon grew into the Carson Valley Inn, a northern Nevada oasis on Highway 395. The Inn opened in 1984 with 100 rooms, a coffee shop, a few slots and a wedding chapel. Today the Carson Valley Inn boasts a 152-room hotel, 75-room motor lodge and 59-site RV resort. It features 650 slot machines, 11 game tables, a poker room, a sports book and 550 employees who excel in customer service and work hard to ensure that your stay is enjoyable. The Inn has also grown to include a coffee bar called Job's Perk and two restaurants, each with its own charm and cuisine. Katie's County Kitchen is a casual coffee shop that serves flavorful café favorites with 24-hour convenience. Fiona's Bar & Grill features a more upscale setting and contemporary culinary offerings plus a bar area and appetizer selection that are ideal for the after-work or post-golf crowd. Guests can take advantage of many other on-site amenities, including a cabaret lounge with nightly live entertainment, a gift shop, massage and facial therapy treatments, a kid's fun center and an indoor pool, spa and fitness area. The quaint wedding chapel along with the meeting and banquet facilities, make it the ideal location for weddings, meetings, corporate retreats and family reunions. The Inn also specializes in group golf packages utilizing 11 area courses and featuring the two courses at the Golf Club at Genoa Lakes. Enjoy all that Nevada has to offer at the Carson Valley Inn.

1627 U.S. Highway 395, Minden NV
(775) 782-9711 or (800) 321-6983 (reservations)
www.cvinn.com

Carpenter's Music World

Music, be it unconscious humming or a full-scale symphony, has been an important part of daily life for as long as there have been people. You can unlock your own musical potential at Carpenter's Music World. At this shop, you can find the instrument that's right for you, plus everything to go with it. Carpenter's Music World stocks pianos of all types, along with nearly every other kind of instrument you can imagine, from trumpets and oboes to xylophones and drum sets. Even those without a musical inclination will be hard-pressed to resist running their fingers across the keys and strings. Carpenter's seeks to help accomplished musicians and budding novices alike. It is staffed by a delightful team of friendly individuals who are dedicated to helping you discover your musical medium. The shop additionally houses a musical academy that provides several classrooms and boasts a cadre of 22 instructors with varying specialties. Carpenter's offers piano tuning, moving and restoration, as well as excellent advice on the care and service of your chosen instrument. Make your contribution to the world of music with a visit to Carpenter's Music World.

6015-G South Virginia Street, Reno NV
(775) 852-7618
www.carpentersmusic.com

St. Mary's Art Center

St. Mary's Art Center (SMAC) is a non-profit organization and school where the atmosphere and accommodations bring talented students together. Many well-known artists have taught or attended classes at SMAC. Artists can sign up for a weekend get-away or a weeklong art class in watercolor, acrylic, oil or pastel. Other class offerings include photography, sculpture, printmaking and creative writing. Camaraderie is guaranteed because you will be lodging with your fellow students right at the center. Built in 1875, the four-story brick structure, originally a Catholic hospital, currently features 15 guest rooms. SMAC has modernized the building, and renovations are a continuing activity. Friends and family are welcome to accompany students if they pay a daily lodging fee. During your stay, you'll enjoy the large upstairs studio, galleries, lounge, kitchen and dining room. When not in the studio, students set up their easels on the lawn, in the surrounding hills or in Virginia City. The blue skies, clean air and incredible light of the high desert can't help but spark creativity. Let St. Mary's Art Center be your place for developing your art and connecting with other artists. Public tours are available during the tourist season, May through October. Please call for more information.

55 North R Street, Virginia City NV
(775) 847-7774
www.stmarysartcenter.org

National Automobile Museum The Harrah Collection

Visitors to the National Automobile Museum learn that every car has a story when they explore decades of intriguing automobiles. The collection includes more than 200 antique, classic and special interest vehicles. Four realistic street scenes, each representing one quarter of the 20th century, house the automobiles. Walk down the Turn of the Century Street, complete with a blacksmith's shop, and see the progression from horse-drawn carriage to cars. Appreciate the beauty of the cars owned by famed Hollywood celebrities, such as James Dean's 1949 Mercury featured in *Rebel Without a Cause* and Elvis Presley's 1973 Cadillac. Learn about the men behind the household names of Buick and Dodge, and how their first inventions were not cars, but bathtubs and bicycles. The museum earns accolades from car buffs and the general public alike. It's ranked in the Top 10 Automobile Museums in the Nation by *Car Collector* magazine and has been named the Best Museum in Northern Nevada by the *Nevada Magazine* Reader's Poll. The Museum Store offers more than 480 automobile-related books, apparel and other memorabilia. Head over to the National Automobile Museum and let your imagination soar.

10 S Lake Street, Reno NV
(775) 333-9300
www.automuseum.org

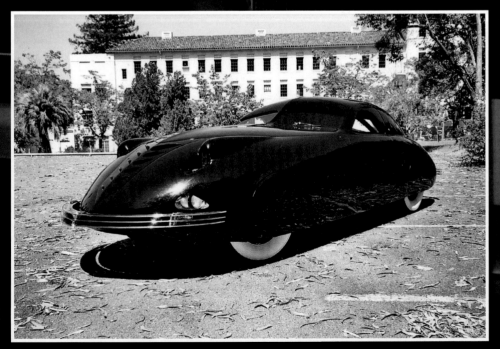

Nevada State Museums

The story of Nevada extends over thousands of years, from the Ice Age through today. Seven Nevada State Museums tell this tale. At the Nevada State Museum, Las Vegas, visitors get a feel for the enormous animals that once roamed the land and walk alongside a full-sized 48-foot carved relief of the ichthyosaur, Nevada's state fossil. Mammoths that disappeared more than 15,000 years ago are brought to life in fascinating displays and exhibits. The first residents of Southern Nevada survived in the desert using amazing skill and resourcefulness. Appreciate the hunting prowess and architectural designs of the Anasazi people at the Lost City Museum in Overton. In Reno, the Nevada Historical Society brings to light the struggles faced by people who have called the region home for the last 13,000 years. Learn the stories of the Carson City Mint, the mining industry and ill-fated ghost towns at the Nevada State Museum in Carson City. The East Ely Railroad Depot Museum and the Nevada State Railroad Museums in Boulder City and Carson City tell of the importance of the railway to the development of the state. Take an excursion train ride along the Boulder Branch Line on vintage Pullman Coaches, or walk through a railroad depot that has remained nearly unchanged since 1907. Hear of the bravery and ingenuity of the people who designed and built the tracks that made Nevada what it is today. Prepare to be mesmerized by Nevada's rich and varied past as you visit each of the seven Nevada State Museums.

700 Twin Lakes Drive, Las Vegas NV
(702) 486-5205 (Nevada State Museum, Las Vegas)

721 S Moapa Valley Boulevard, Overton NV
(702) 397-2193 (Lost City Museum)

1650 N Virginia Street, Reno NV
(775) 688-1190 (Nevada Historical Society)

600 N Carson Street, Carson City NV
(775) 687-4810 (Nevada State Museum)

1100 Avenue A, Ely NV
(775) 289-1663 (East Ely Railroad Depot Museum)

600 Yucca Street, Boulder City NV
(702) 486-5933 (Nevada State Railroad Museum)

2180 S Carson Street, Carson City NV
(775) 687-6953 (Nevada State Railroad Museum)

www.nevadaculture.org

Hot August Nights

The sight of sparkling classic cars mixes with the sounds of classic 1950s and 1960s rock n' roll to create a one-of-a-kind experience during Hot August Nights in Reno and Sparks. Hot August Nights, held during the first full week of August, is the largest classic car show and nostalgia event in the world, drawing more than 800,000 visitors each year. Attendees come from all across the United States, as well as Britain, Australia, Germany and many other countries. The event, which features more than 10,000 classic cars from 1972 and earlier, is so large it is housed at six sites. Show n' shine competitions take place daily and of course there are cruises every night. *Car & Driver* magazine has named the event as the number one classic car show anywhere. Hot August Nights also features a swap meet where hobbyists who restore classic cars can trade parts. The Big Boys Toy Store offers all the latest in aftermarket products. If you're looking for a new project, check out the Silver Auctions, which have sold more than 1,000 primo classic cars. Hot August Nights goes beyond passenger cars, with a Stars and Stripes Truckerfest that showcases 18-wheeler trucks of the 1950s and 1960s in a neon light parade. Icons of the early rock 'n roll era put on free performances. Rock the night away at the Prom and Sock Hop. You'll also find craft fairs and exhibitions, a corporate exhibition village on everything to do with cars, a poker run and walk, and a 5,000-car parade on the last day of the event. Lace up your blue suede shoes and cruise on over to Hot August Nights for some of the finest cars and music ever made.

1425 E Greg Street, Sparks NV
(775) 356-1956
www.hotaugustnights.net

Photo by Naomi West

Photo by Atsushi Fujimori

Photo by Mikael Forslund

Photo by Kevin Grantham

Photo by Ed Anderson

National Championship Air Races

In 2007, the National Championship Air Races celebrates its 44th annual event. Be sure to wear a hat and plenty of sun block, because you are going to spend much of your time looking straight up into a clear Nevada sky, where six classes of aircraft thunder overhead, breaking old speed records and setting new ones. Air racing is the world's fastest motor sport with planes in the unlimited class reaching speeds of 500 miles per hour. Each year, the event is chock full of talented pilots who perform military and civil flight demonstrations. The Canadian Snowbirds dazzle the crowds with their aerobatic performances. Every pilot at this event is a superhero who performs death-defying feats to thrill hundreds of thousands of visitors. A ground display of aircraft also intrigues the crowd. You can climb into a military cargo plane, visit the pilots and watch race teams work on the aircraft. Along with food and beverages, visitors browse for aviation-related merchandise, including official National Championship Air Race mementos. In recent years, the five-day show, held in mid-September, has taken place at the Reno Stead Airfield about eight miles north of Reno off Route 395. You can follow the cars to the low-cost auto parking and reserved RV parking at the race site or take a low-fare round-trip shuttle from several points in downtown Reno to the event grounds. For air entertainment that will keep you on the edge of your seat, attend the National Championship Air Races.

Stead Boulevard, Reno Stead Airfield, Reno NV
(775) 972-6663
www.airrace.org

Photo by Brad Powell

Lake Tahoe Shakespeare Festival

Where else can you enjoy Shakespeare on the beach and under the stars, but at the Lake Tahoe Shakespeare Festival? Set at the scenic Sand Harbor State Park outdoor amphitheatre, the Lake Tahoe Shakespeare Festival brings the Bard to life each summer. The annual six-week season begins mid-July and runs seven nights per week featuring a medley of Shakespeare's greatest works plus the occasional modern and contemporary addition, with a balanced mix of comedy and drama. The Festival also boasts Shakespeare's Kitchen, a newly remodeled food and beverage area located inside the theater gates that offers an assortment of dining options. The Festival is also focused on introducing the wonders of theater to children of all ages. Each season, The D.G. Menchetti Young Shakespeare Program offers free matinees at Sand Harbor, as well as theaters around the region. The educational outreach program also extends to schools with a highly interactive theater workshop series. The Lake Tahoe Shakespeare Festival has been presented with numerous awards including Best of Nevada: North by *Nevada Magazine*, the Tourism Development award from the State of Nevada, Best Production of a Shakespeare Play by the *Sacramento News & Review* and Local Secret, Big Finds by Travelocity. A range of ticket prices and seating sections are available each season. For more information or to order tickets, call or visit the website. The Lake Tahoe Shakespeare Festival is coordinated by 40 professional staff and approximately 200 volunteers each season.

948 Incline Way, Incline Village NV
775-832-1616
www.LakeTahoeShakespeare.com

The Great Reno Balloon Race

During three days in early September, you can look up into the Reno skies and see a rainbow of hot air balloons soaring about. From its humble beginnings in 1982 with just 20 balloons, The Great Reno Balloon Race has taken flight with more than 100 balloons each year. More than 140,000 people attended the race in 2006, and those numbers are expected to rise, just like the balloons themselves. The race features several events, including a Hare & Hound competition, in which pilots chase two so-called hare balloons to their ultimate destination and try to strike a laid-out target. In the Judge Declared Goal competition, pilots fly to a destination chosen by the judges based on the prevailing winds. This being Nevada, there's even a Balloon Blackjack Tournament, in which pilots toss beanbags down on giant playing cards. Spectators will marvel at the early-morning Dawn Patrol, which features a handful of balloonists qualified to fly in the dark. The balloons twinkle, glow and fly along with choreographed music. Visit Balloon Boulevard, where a wide array of souvenirs and crafts are for sale, in addition to warm food and drink. Don't forget to bring your camera to help capture the memories of this one-of-a-kind experience. If you're looking for an aerial event that will leave you with a sky-high feeling, come to The Great Reno Balloon Race.

Reno NV
(775) 826-1181
www.renoballoon.com

Reno Philharmonic Association

The Reno Philharmonic Association's mission is to provide world-class, innovative musical performances and exceptional educational and outreach programs that attract the widest possible audience. The orchestra, made up of more than 60 local and talented musicians, performs in various venues in Reno and throughout northern Nevada and California under the leadership of Music Director and Conductor Barry Jekowsky. The popular MasterClassics Series is performed from September to April. The orchestra also presents more than 10 specialty performances such as the holiday classic, Spirit of the Season. It also presents Rhythm and Rawhide, 4th of July in Genoa, Broadway on the Beach at Sand Harbor and the annually sold out Pops on the River. The Philharmonic's impressive and diverse education department includes two youth orchestras, a series of eight Young People's Concerts performed throughout the school year, Celebrate Strings, an in-school violin instruction program and a Discover Music program, which brings music ensembles into schools. The orchestra has received special recognition in recent years, including the Best of Reno award from *Reno Magazine* in 2006 and Best Performing Arts Group in Reno nine times from 1991 to 2001 by *Reno Gazette-Journal* readers. The Philharmonic and the Reno Philharmonic Guild have been honored to receive several Silver Star awards for education programs and concerts from Truckee Meadows Tomorrow. In 2003, the Reno Philharmonic Youth Orchestras received a Best of Reno award from the editors and readers of the *Reno News and Review*.

925 Riverside Drive, Suite 3, Reno NV (775) 323-6393
www.renophilharmonic.com

Photo by Tim Torell

Photo by Tim Torell

Animal Ark Wildlife Sanctuary & Nature Center

Set on 38 secluded acres just northwest of Reno, Animal Ark is a nonprofit sanctuary for animals that can no longer be released into their native habitats. Animal Ark provides these creatures with a realistic, stimulating environment while offering visitors the chance to see and learn about them. Glass viewing areas, live animal exhibits and educational displays help to educate the public about bears, mountain lions, wolves, cheetahs, tigers and many other species that make their home at the sanctuary and nature center. Visitors learn the story of each animal and the importance of predators to healthy ecosystems. Docents and educators are available to answer any questions the guests may have in addition to offering general assistance throughout the park. Several annual events at the facility, such as Wolf Howl Night, Cheetah Challenge, Ark after Dark, Harvest Festival and more, are highly attended events that offer as much entertainment to the animals as to the people. Along with enjoying a wild experience with nature, visitors will find a beautifully designed, well-stocked gift shop, secluded picnic tables and, with prior arrangements, guides for groups of 20 or more. Visit Animal Ark for a rare opportunity to meet wildlife ambassadors that represent their wild cousins. With its natural habitat exhibits tucked into the rolling hills, the Ark is a place for peaceful reflection on our world and the creatures with which we share it. Animal Ark is out in the country, so be sure to dial 1 when you call.

1265 Deerlodge Road, Reno NV
(off Red Rock Road via Highway 395 N from Reno)
(775) 970-3111
www.animalark.org

The Fourth Ward School

In the year of America's centennial celebration, the people of Virginia City began building an imposing structure to educate a thousand schoolchildren. The Fourth Ward School, built in Second Empire architectural style, stands at the south entrance to the city and offers an important reminder of the value of education to this 19th century mining town. The city lavished state-of-the-art features on the structure, which housed a visionary approach to what we would today call multi-cultural education. In 1936, the school closed and remained unoccupied until 50 years later, when it opened as a community center and museum. Visitors can now view artifacts and gain insight into the historic events of the Comstock Lode. Groups can rent space at the school for affordable prices. The 100-seat E.L. Wiegland Great Hall was restored to its original state in 2001 and handles receptions, meetings and luncheons. A grammar school classroom, furnished with original desks, suits small workshops. Another classroom offers exhibit space, and still another describes Comstock mining. In 2004, the inspirational building won the National Preservation Honor Award. Visit the historic Fourth Ward School, a building that celebrates the quest for a better life in the Wild West.

537 South C Street, Virginia City NV
(775) 847-0975
www.fourthwardschool.org

Belle's Tea Cottage

Remember playing dress-up and having tea parties with your favorite teddy bear? Belle's Tea Cottage in Reno brings back that magic with tea parties of the grown-up variety. At Belle's, you can enjoy a lunch of homemade soup, quiche or salad under tea cup chandeliers. Traditional afternoon tea features organic tea from Davidson's Tea Company of Nevada and a background of classical music. Owners Clara "Belle" Knight and Logan Knight recognize that a tea room should be a place to enjoy a great cup of tea and good conversation with friends. Each day features a different selection of teas as well as teas for children, iced tea and lemonade. Pair your tea with finger sandwiches and tasty desserts for a pleasant mix of English tradition and Western hospitality. Elegant, high tea is served all day. Staff can take your photo as a souvenir, and the gift shop provides local and imported tea-related gifts. Belle's is ideal for such celebrations as bridal and baby showers. You can treat the special little girl in your life to a birthday tea party, which includes a special decaffeinated children's tea served on elegant tea trays in their very own party room. Children dress up in hats and feather boas and enjoy an etiquette class. The birthday girl receives a special teacup and a souvenir photo. Gather your friends and family for an old-fashioned tea at Belle's Tea Cottage.

1635 Marvel Way, Reno NV
(775) 826-3006
www.belles-tea-cottage.com

Sweetie Pies by Wendy

Wendy Smith's husband dislikes cake but loves pie, so Wendy became very good at baking pies, the kind with flaky pastry and fresh fillings. Once they taste the goods at Sweetie Pies by Wendy, customers agree that pie is the world's most perfect dessert. In 2002, Wendy quit her job with GE to pursue the pie business. Before beginning, she tested her ability to handle a production pace at a local cookie bakery. Slowly, word of Wendy's pies spread as she struck up deals with local restaurants and donated her product to local fundraisers and mixers. Wendy's dream of a retail store became a reality when she opened her first shop in 2003. In 2005 she moved the shop to its Minden Village location. Wendy even designed her own kitchen and décor. Wendy bakes every day and sometimes gets help from family. You can walk in and sample what's in the display case or order ahead to assure the pie of your choice, perhaps apple, peach, lemon meringue, maple pecan, strawberry rhubarb or chocolate cream. Not all of Wendy's pies are sweet. Her pot pies and quiches make satisfying family meals. In the same spirit of old-fashioned goodness, Wendy bakes brownies and cookies, but no cakes. Try a pie at Sweetie Pies by Wendy, and you may never eat cake again.

1663 Lucerne Street, Suite A, Minden NV (775) 782-6633

Classical Glass

If it's true that artists put a part of themselves into everything they create, then a little bit of Becky Soderman hangs in homes throughout the United States. She has even sold her stained glass creations to customers from Europe and Canada. Classical Glass is on Main Street in historic downtown Gardnerville, right next to the Overland Hotel and Basque Restaurant in the city's first brick fire house. Stained glass windows are Becky's specialty. She invites you to come in and see her latest works of beauty, including the stained glass wedding gifts that have made her studio famous. Becky also offers classes in making stained glass windows. She was a potter before she fell under the spell of glass back in the 1970s. She opened Classical Glass in 1982 as a gallery and working studio. It has since evolved into an eclectic gift shop as well, featuring exquisitely crafted art and a fine collection of silver and crystal jewelry from all over the world. Discover the alluring fragrances of Zents, an entire line of all-natural personal care products in 12 delicious scents. Other highlights include cards, music, candles and home décor. New items come in everyday and Becky and Kati are constantly changing displays for every season. In short, you will find gifts for everyone on your list at Classical Glass, which promises shopping with an uptown flair in downtown Gardnerville. Watch the artisans at work and shop for pretty things to take home to your corner of the world at Classical Glass.

1453 U.S. Highway 395, Gardnerville NV
(775) 782-5830

Art Source, More Than a Gallery

Art Source, More Than a Gallery is a source for ideas, where every piece of art represents a possible way to enhance or set the tone of a room. As soon as you step inside this Reno gallery, you are surrounded by beauty in the form of a seemingly endless collection of American landscapes, Western scenes, European etchings and Asian artwork. Figurative and abstract images for your walls, sculpture and glass—you will find it all in this gallery with its museum-size inventory. Often similar works are displayed together to show how you might use them to unify the look of your home or business. "We are not a trendy gallery," says owner Christel Citko. "We offer artwork that is timeless, and we offer true value." Christel is aware that for many people shopping for art means hunting for the lowest price on the Internet. "Value is different from low price," she points out. "Low price often means low quality, no service and no extras. Value means quality, knowledge and service." Christel offers homeowners and businesses value pricing on artwork and framing. Art Source is Northern Nevada's only state-of-the-art design and custom framing center, featuring Picture-It-First, which lets you see the product framed before you purchase it. She takes her responsibility to the community seriously by offering partnerships in philanthropy. Ask her how your purchases may benefit the Nevada Humane Society, Animal Ark, the Wilbur D. May Arboretum, SPCA and the Boys & Girls Club of Truckee Meadows while providing a tax benefit for you. For ideas on how to fill any space with beauty, visit Art Source.

9748 S Virginia Street, Reno NV
(775) 828-3525
www.artsourcereno.com

Photos by Tom Robinson

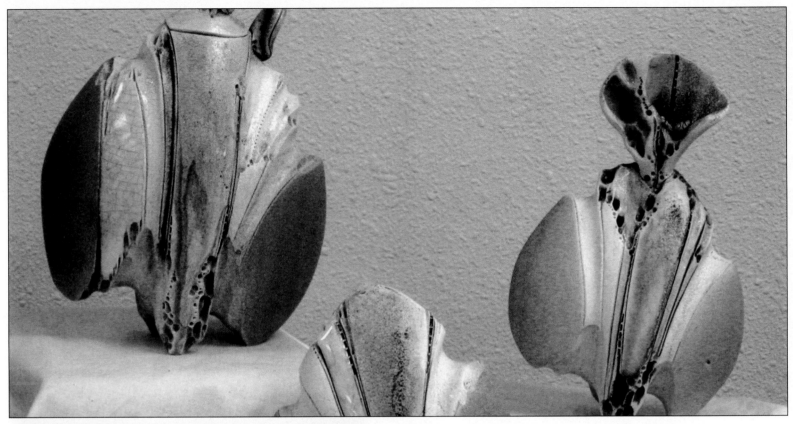

Artisans International Gallery

If you appreciate art and are curious about world cultures, then shopping at Artisans International Gallery is likely to be the highlight of your Minden experience. All nations under one roof is a good description of the store, because owner Bronwyn Mason has assembled an exciting array of native arts from all over the globe. You can start with jewelry from New Zealand and Poland, work your way through the metal wall art and Polish gobelins, and continue with special pieces from Peru, Argentina, Madagascar, Nepal, Indonesia and many other exotic locales. You will end up marveling over beaded animals and dolls from South Africa. The art at Artisans International Gallery is created using every material imaginable, including glass, clay and fiber as well as wood, wire and metal. When asked how she chooses the merchandise, Bronwyn says, "I look for artists who work in the traditional techniques of their country but create work with a contemporary view." She enjoys supporting businesses and cooperatives that empower native peoples. An example is MonkeyBiz, which employs 450 disadvantaged women in Cape Town, who use traditional beadwork to make animals in a variety of sizes and a spectrum of colors. "There is something for everyone at Artisans International," says Bronwyn. Customers tell her they are buying pieces for their own collections in addition to birthday gifts and other special occasions. Shop globally for native arts at Artisans International Gallery.

1653 Lucerne Street, Suite B, Minden NV (775) 783-8881
www.artisansinternationalinc.com

Planet X Pottery

Since 1974, art lovers looking for one of the most unique pottery studios and galleries in the solar system have headed to Planet X—Planet X Pottery, that is. John and Rachel Bogard own and operate the studio, which is located at the foot of Granite Mountain between the Smoke Creek and Black Rock deserts of northern Nevada. John has crafted pottery since 1969 and has studied with the renowned Al Johnsen at the University of California, Santa Cruz. John's wife, Rachel, was a veterinarian before making the journey to Planet X. The gallery offers an impressive array of pottery, including fine porcelain pieces, stoneware and raku. All the more impressive, the studio is completely off the electrical grid. Power comes exclusively from an array of solar panels and propane tanks. In addition to offering a popular Open House, Show & Sale on Memorial Day weekend and in September, the Bogards offer their wares at a show in Reno the first weekend of December. If you're looking for an out-of-this-world selection of beautiful pottery, blast off for Planet X Pottery.

8100 Highway 447, Gerlach NV
(775) 557-2500
www.planetxpottery.com

Argenta Earth & Fire Company

Mimi Patrick has spent the past decade creating utilitarian stoneware and porcelain art. Her gallery and studio, Argenta Earth & Fire Company, is open most days, unless the fishing is very good. Mimi challenges herself to explore new forms for the house and garden. She seeks inspiration from the natural world and uses the shapes of animals and birds in her one-of-a-kind creations. She employs a potter's wheel for most pieces, but adds many hand-built components. Some pots have carved wood handles. Others use metal, shell, bone or turquoise knobs. Mimi is deeply aware of the merging of earth and fire that pottery entails. She chooses clays for their specific qualities and then fires an updraft gas kiln to 2,400 degrees Fahrenheit. Her fiery cat, Schizo, adds a paw print now and again. The glazes are lead-free, and the pottery is safe for use in the microwave, dishwasher and oven. Mimi also produces woodcarvings, which use found objects and express folk art themes. She works in a vintage schoolhouse in Gold Canyon, where miners found the gold that led to the discovery of the Comstock Lode. Whether you seek functional pottery for everyday use or organic shapes for decorative purposes, visit Argenta Earth & Fire Company, just a mile from Virginia City.

1631 Main Street, Gold Hill NV
(775) 847-7466
www.nevpotter.com

Richardson Gallery of Fine Art

Mark Richardson credits Dr. Seuss for getting him hooked on art when he was just two years old. Mark's taste for the whimsical is still strong, as a visit to his Richardson Gallery of Fine Art in Reno would prove, although his range has definitely expanded to include everything from serene Impressionist landscapes to chic conceptual creations. Mark claims that his is the largest international gallery in the area, a showcase for paintings as well as sculpture and art glass. Art that you can touch, such as tables and chairs, is another specialty here. Mark, who was an art collector and dealer for many years prior to opening his gallery, regularly scouts the world for exceptional pieces. About half of the works on display are originals, and about half are limited editions. Mark works with established artists and also likes to take chances on up and coming talents. Ask him to name a favorite, and he'll reveal that he was overjoyed to feature the works of Dr. Seuss in a special exhibit that drew a whole new clientele to his gallery. Take your love of art to the Richardson Gallery of Fine Art.

3670 S Virginia Street, Reno NV
(725) 828-0888
www.richardsonfineart.com

Steamboat Hot Springs Healing Center & Spa

Wash away your physical ailments and heal the bruises of life at Steamboat Hot Springs Healing Center & Spa in Reno. Experience a natural geothermal mineral bath in one of seven private tub rooms, each using a drain-and-fill system that pipes the water from the hot springs, giving each new visitor a fresh, chemical-free experience. Enjoy the five-person outdoor tub, which uses a water-flow-through system that allows you to soothe aching joints, heal injuries or just wash away worries and stress with the benefits of sulfate and other rare minerals. Of course, the breathtaking backdrop of the Sierra Nevada Mountains doesn't hurt either. Other offerings include therapeutic massage, mud treatments, facials, hot stone, raindrop and acoustic therapy. The spa offers three therapeutic massage rooms, a facials room, natural geothermal steam room and an acoustic therapy room, which uses many sound frequencies to treat imbalances in the body. All therapies focus on health with an emphasis on physical and emotional healing with natural light and color therapy. Steamboat is the oldest known site with continuous hot spring activity and mineral deposit production in the United States. Most believe Mark Twain named the retreat when he said, "Behold a steamboat in the desert." Come nurture your body and mind at Steamboat Hot Springs.

16010 S Virginia Street, Reno NV
(775) 853-6600
www.steamboatsprings.org

Genesis Salon & Medical Spa

Genesis Salon & Medical Spa is Northern Nevada's largest and most complete spa facility, offering a full range of cosmetic services. The independent medical experts at Genesis provide truly amazing results for overall skin enhancement. The staff members are trained and certified in all treatments offered, and operate above the highest standards required by the state. Complimentary consultations are provided to educate clients about anti-aging and skin refinement programs and defining a course of treatment. Treatments include photo rejuvenation, laser hair removal, vein therapy, intense pulsed light, red LED light treatment, blue LED light therapy, skin peels, and Botox and Restylane treatments. The equipment used at Genesis includes the latest, most advanced precision medical devices available today. By choosing Genesis, you can be confident that treatments meet the highest standards, and produce noticeable results. The salon at Genesis offers the latest in hair styling techniques, skin and body treatments including hair extensions and color, massages, reflexology and body wraps. Genesis offers the best hair and skin products available, including Bumble and Bumble, IS Clinical, I mage, Obaji, Glymed and Jane Iredell. Genesis also offers full service wedding packages for the entire bridal party to make that special day a relaxing journey that's worry and stress free, including a trial run for hair and make-up at a discounted price. Genesis Salon & Medical Spa has created the perfect environment for that pampering getaway.

250 Crummer Lane, Reno NV
(775) 828-9797
www.genesissalon.com

Hall & Wrye Plastic Surgeons

At Hall & Wrye Plastic Surgeons, two respected Reno surgeons offer surgical and non-surgical procedures to patients who wish to improve their appearance. Drs. Wesley Hall, Jr. and Scott Wrye and their longtime staff have worked together as a team for many years and share a respect for your comfort and concerns. They honor the office slogan: Here is the one time in your life when it's all about you. The doctors stress that your decision to have plastic surgery is not about your partner, your mother or the people you meet in the street. They insist that the focus remain on you and your needs throughout the decision-making process and throughout all treatments and surgeries. They provide plenty of opportunities for you to ask questions, including a second consultation free of charge. You will receive a written quote and detailed instructions. Lab tests are performed on the premises. Breast surgeries include augmentation, lifts, reduction and reconstruction. Facial services include full and mini face-lifts and rhinoplasty. You can also receive body contouring following extreme weight loss, tummy tucks and liposuction. Non-surgical procedures include the thread lift, an alternative to a face-lift, and several procedures for reducing wrinkles and spider veins. An aesthetician adds still more beautifying therapies. For honest advice and state-of-the-art procedures, visit Hall & Wrye Plastic Surgeons.

635 Sierra Rose Drive, Reno NV
(775) 829-6564
www.hallandwrye.com

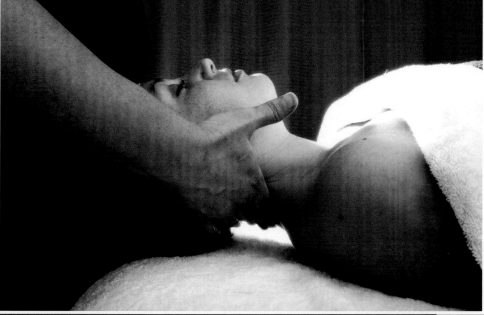

Photos by Jessi LeMay

Bodies in Balance

Create well-being and heal your body from within using the ancient Japanese art of Seifukujutsu at Bodies in Balance. Owner Tammi Odell specializes in the Japanese restoration therapy at her Reno facility. Henry Sheshiro Okazaki first brought the therapy to Hawaii from Japan in the 1940s. Healers in Japan have used the method for more than 1,200 years to bring the body into balance with a combination of massage, reflexology, auricular therapy and the five elements. Tammi's education includes more than 1,400 hours of training under Professor Ken Eddy in this special therapy, as well as an apprenticeship in Swedish massage under Barbara Wall. Tammi's nurturing personality immediately puts clients at ease and is one of the reasons her services are sought after by local obstetricians and pregnant patients. She offers prenatal massages and attends labors and deliveries to help mothers-to-be stay relaxed and encourage bonding between mom and the new baby. Clients come to Bodies in Balance for help in treating a variety of conditions, and have found relief from the symptoms of fibromyalgia, migraines, diabetes and other ailments that make it difficult to perform daily tasks. Visit Bodies in Balance to relax and restore your body.

3745 Wagoneer Drive, Reno NV
(775) 815-4263

G & G Nursery and Landscaping

More than 20 years of landscape experience, world travels and love of the Sparks area culminate in the lush gardens and amazing designs at G & G Nursery and Landscaping. In the 1970s, father and son owners John and Steve Giossi opened a nursery that quickly became known as a great place to go for a large selection of quality plants and friendly service. As the nursery gained popularity, John and Steve began searching for a larger piece of land, where they could really showcase their landscaping abilities. After looking for many years, G & G Nursery moved to its new location in 2006, and the Giossis knew that this was the spot they had been waiting for. Now, they have space to showcase a myriad of ideas for customers to incorporate into their own backyards. Walk through the grounds on a variety of pavers, enjoy the sounds of water features, and choose from a huge selection of plants and shrubbery, many of which are grown by John's other son, Kevin, on his land in California. G & G's landscape services transform even the most barren piece of Nevada desert into an oasis, and the gift shop offers a range of home and garden décor, from delicate vases to wall hangings and other treasures from around the world. If you are tired of the view out of your window, come to G & G Nursery and Landscaping to create a welcoming outdoor space.

3397 Pyramid Way, Sparks NV
(775) 358-1700

Juniper Hill Furniture and Accessories

If you consider yourself a witty person, then why choose a dull couch for your living room? However you define who you are, the folks at Juniper Hill Furniture and Accessories can help you fill your home according to your own personal style. "We're all different," say owners Trish and David Dietze. Trish's fashion sense guides her in putting together not only rooms but entire homes for clients. She aids them with color palette, full design and set up. Do you want your home to say *you*? Then give Trish and David six hours of your time. That's right, they'll have a home fully furnished and ready for its owners in that amount of time. Their store carries not only furniture but beautiful bedding and accessories down to the smallest detail, such as candles for the mantel and placemats for the table. The furniture, linens and draperies are the finest imports from all over the world. The Dietzes began the store as something to do after retirement. A few years later, they are open seven days a week and employ 30 people. Readers of *Reno Magazine* recently gave Juniper Hill their vote of approval for Best Furniture in the area. Don't just buy furniture for your home, make a personal statement with the help of the staff at Juniper Hill Furniture and Accessories.

850 E Patriot Boulevard, Reno NV
(775) 853-8300
www.juniperhillfurniture.com

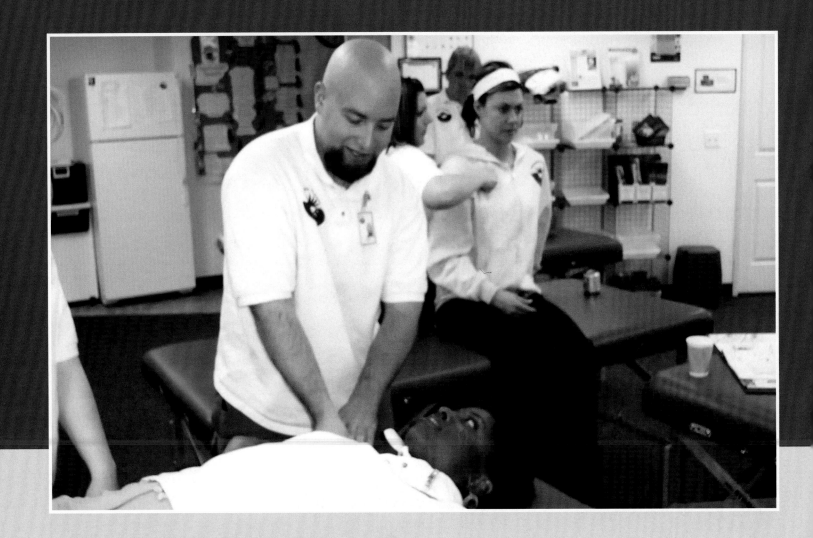

Ralston School of Massage

As Nevada's oldest licensed massage school, Ralston School of Massage celebrates its 20th anniversary in 2008. Its ongoing commitment is to help every student establish a solid foundation based on the essential fundamentals of massage therapy. As a student, you learn the functions of the human body and scientific theories about why massage works. You learn and perform a combination of proven massage techniques developed through years of successful practice. You also learn business skills needed to succeed whether starting your own business or working as an employee. From this secure foundation, you can build a successful massage therapy career. Offering morning, afternoon or evening classes, students may complete the program in as little as nine to 11 months for full-time and 14 to 16 months for part-time. The 710-hour program offers each student the skills necessary to move from school into a rewarding profession. In 2006, graduates had a 100 percent pass rate on the National Certification Exam. When you're ready to begin an exciting new career in massage therapy, call for a full catalog. Ralston School of Massage also offers an affordable student massage clinic to the public. Call today and enjoy the wonderful benefits of massage therapy.

5605 Riggins Court, Suite 201, Reno NV
(775) 827-1800
www.ralstonmassage.com

Tahoe Dave's Skis and Boards

Lake Tahoe is famous for many things, not the least of which is the spectacular skiing and snowboarding that the long winters and steep mountains generously afford. If a long run down the perfect powdery slope is what you're in the market for, there's no better place than Tahoe Dave's Skis and Boards to outfit you in style. The establishment rents quality equipment and apparel for both novice and experienced snow enthusiasts, and owner Dave Wilderotter knows how to keep his customers happy after 30 years in business. Tahoe Dave's offers rental packages and specials to fit every need. All locations offer children's equipment, so your little ski bunnies can join in on some family fun. Skiers or boarders with long-term rentals can opt to bring their equipment back in each evening for re-waxing at no extra charge. Dave and Manager Marina Marenco strive to keep the rental process as smooth and enjoyable as possible and even offer an extra 15 percent discount to anyone willing to sing the University of Michigan fight song—loudly—in tribute to Dave's alma mater. Equipment can be rented and returned at any Tahoe Dave's, including the two Tahoe City stores and stores in Truckee, Olympic Valley and Kings Beach. Be sure to call ahead or check the website for variations in hours. When winter rolls around and you find yourself in the stunning Sierra mountain range surrounding Lake Tahoe, make Tahoe Dave's Skis and Boards your first stop on the way to memorable winter fun.

590 N Lake Boulevard, Tahoe City CA (530) 583-6415
600 N Lake Boulevard, Tahoe City CA (530) 583-0400
10200 Donner Pass Road, Truckee CA (530) 582-0900
8299 N Lake Boulevard, Kings Beach CA (530) 546-5800
3039 Highway 89, Olympic Valley CA (530) 583-5669
www.tahoedaves.com

Photos by Jeff Lamppert

Soar Minden

The gliders of Soar Minden have been a familiar sight in the sky above Lake Tahoe since 1978. Unless you're a bird, a silent flight over the lake is possible only in one of these soaring craft. Soar Minden offers several High Sierra excursions, including the breathtaking 20-minute Lake Tahoe Ride and an hour-long aerial cruise that provides excellent photo opportunities of Emerald Bay and Fallen Leaf Lake. Both can accommodate one or two passengers. Acrobatic flights featuring loops and wingovers are available for those with a stout heart and nerves of steel. If you would rather be a captain than a passenger, the flight school at Soar Minden offers a single introductory lesson as well as comprehensive instruction leading to a glider license. Minden is a magical place for sailplane enthusiasts, the equivalent of Aspen for skiers or Pebble Beach for golfers. Perfect thermals and updrafts produce what many consider to be the world's greatest soaring conditions. Many gliding records for high altitude and long distance have been set in the area. The feeling that you get from silent flight is nothing short of sublime. Come soar with the eagles aboard a Soar Minden glider.

1138 Airport Road, Minden NV
(775) 782-7627 or (800) 345-7627
www.soarminden.com

Classic Adventures RV Rentals

If your idea of the perfect vacation is an open road and the ultimate in mobile luxury, Classic Adventures RV Rentals in Reno has you in mind. With a reputation 25 years strong, the business is owned by the Miles family and operated by General Manager Erik Schultz, who makes a firm commitment to quality and service. The company can put you in a smaller class C vehicle, mid-sized class A or a specialty diesel luxury coach. All of the available motor homes are made by Winnebago, the industry's leading name in recreational vehicles, and all come equipped with a full array of amenities, including luxury bedding and towels, quality kitchenware, satellite television, Sirius satellite radio and DVD players. Safety is a priority at Classic Adventures, where all rentals include 24-hour roadside assistance along with back-up cameras, electric steps and generators. Rental rates are similar to average hotel rates and vary according to season. The rates are straightforward without a lot of added-on expense. Classic Adventures also rents light-weight travel trailers (see the website for more information). The staff is happy to assist in mapping out your entire vacation, so grab the family, some groceries and other essentials and head to Classic Adventures RV Rentals and answer the call of the open road.

2802 Kietzke Lane, Reno NV
(775) 825-1200 or (866) 825-8141
www.classicadventuresrv.com

Adele's Restaurant & Lounge

Great restaurants are a labor of love. Why else would anyone devote the countless hours needed to create a place that diners return to again and again? At Adele's Restaurant & Lounge, owner and Chef Charlie Abowd takes pride in serving the finest food with impeccable service. His creativity and commitment to fresh ingredients has earned recognition from *Nevada Magazine* and *Wine Spectator*. Adele's has received the Award of Excellence from the Distinguished Restaurants of North America, bestowed only upon establishments of the highest quality. There are no short cuts in Charlie's kitchen. His creative continental menu features more than 75 diverse items and a dozen daily specials. The wine list contains 170 carefully chosen selections. Appetizers include escargot, caviar and boutique cheeses. Maryland soft shell crabs are prepared in several ways. The oyster bar is a must. Main courses include certified natural beef, pork and duck, highlighted with thoughtfully prepared sauces that enhance the natural flavors of each dish. Charlie has a penchant for lamb and offers several lamb entrées. He makes a terrific seafood jambalaya, among other Louisiana specialties. For dessert, try the rich crème brûlée or sample the New Orleans bread pudding. Charlie is a third-generation restaurateur. His parents, Paul and Adele, opened Adele's in 1977. Charlie joined his parents in 1980, and in 1998 he bought the restaurant with his wife, Karen. Experience Adele's Restaurant & Lounge, where nothing less than the best is acceptable.

1112 N Carson Street, Carson City NV
(775) 882-3353
www.adelerestaurantandlounge.com

G-G's Mahogany Grill

When you step into G-G's Mahogany Grill, you will immediately be treated to the smell of mahogany and the promise of a delightful meal. Owners Steve Melancon and Sandra Triglia named their restaurant after Grandma Gloria and her husband, Guy, who ran the old Christmas Tree restaurant on Mount Rose Highway in the 1950s. Experience the large-portion steaks, chops and other standards once enjoyed by Marilyn Monroe, Rosemary Clooney and Michael Landon. Elegant appetizers, a generous selection of soup and salads, plus seafood and pasta dishes round out the Christmas Tree's original menu. Save room for such desserts as crème brûlée and tiramisu. Repeat customers benefit from a member's card that entitles them to discounts and special promotions. The interior is one of casual elegance and history. Wood and brick coupled with comfortable banquet tables invite you to relax and enjoy good company and great food. Bar seating is also available for times when you want to enjoy lighter fare or one of the available wines or other libations. Old newspaper stories line the walls of the bar area, showing Grandma with her locally famous tiger and bear, who used to live outside the restaurant in large cages. With such local history, it's no wonder Steve and Sandra named their restaurant after Gloria and Guy. For a charming meal steeped in history, come to G-G's Mahogany Grill.

8175 S Virginia, Reno NV (775) 853-2266

210 North

With its retro-riffic look and elegant big city nightclub feel, 210 North is a prime destination for those stepping out in style. This Reno nightclub, lounge and restaurant features 17,500 square feet of space, including three bars and two VIP rooms. Owners Rob Stone and Jill Gianoli opened the club in 2006 after years of planning. That planning has paid off in one of the swankiest clubs you're likely to find outside of New York or San Francisco. One of the first things that will catch your eye is the enormous chandelier that hangs in 210 North. Designed by artist Eva Menz, the chandelier features 4,000 handmade glass pieces hanging from six miles of cable. The bars are fitted with white marble, and the dance floor will literally change colors beneath your feet as you groove to the latest tunes. You'll find a variety of music on the menu here, including "everything from Brazilian to Flamenco to funk and soul," according to Jill. After dancing the night away, guests can rest on the elegant custom-made furniture here, which even includes beds. The fancy marble bar serves up a full variety of fancy drinks, mixed to perfection. Beginning in mid 2007, Mediterraneo, the club's restaurant, will serve an array of tapas and small plates from around the Mediterranean. Get dressed to the nines and have an evening that will rank as a Perfect 10 at 210 North.

210 N Sierra Street, Reno NV
(775) 786-6210
www.210north.com

Photos by Kiley Howard

Red's Little Waldorf Saloon

A beer with friends and a cheer for the Wolf Pack have been traditions at Red's Little Waldorf Saloon since 1922. Since this Reno landmark opened its doors as the Little Waldorf all those years ago, it has been a top location for University of Nevada students and alumni to gather for fun, food and drink. The saloon was recently purchased and refurbished with wagons, cannons and other Western memorabilia hanging on the walls. You'll also find plenty of Wolf Pack memorabilia, including football programs from the 1980s. One of the big changes at the saloon has been the addition of delicious barbeque, made famous at Red's Old 395 Grill in Carson City. Enjoy a generous rack of ribs, a smoked half chicken or a pulled pork sandwich. You'll also find numerous hamburgers, salads and sandwiches as well as freshly made pizzas. Red's is certain to satisfy your thirst with more than 50 different beers, fine wines and premium spirits. Red's Little Waldorf Saloon keeps everyone amused with two pool tables and a video arcade for the whole family to enjoy. Red's also offers catering services. Come to Red's Little Waldorf Saloon to raise your glass to the Wolf Pack while you enjoy tasty food and drinks with your friends.

1661 N Virginia Street, Reno NV
(775) 337-9255

Red's Old 395 Grill

The flavors and sites of the Old West are on full display at Red's Old 395 Grill. The scent of smoky barbecue, slathered in the restaurant's one-of-a-kind Howlin' Coyote barbeque sauce, will start your mouth watering from the moment you walk in. The Carson City ambience here includes a décor featuring farm wagons, mining tools and old-time pictures; a 1923 Monarch Steamroller lends rustic charm. Look for two-pound St. Louis-style ribs, smoked double pork chops and three types of sausage along with house-made coleslaw. The portions here are huge. Other entrees that win praise are the wood-fired salmon, grilled rib-eye steak and chicken piccata. Red's Old 395 Grill has won Best of Carson for their tender, juicy steaks. Pizza lovers will delight in the variety here, baked fresh in a wood-fire oven. Red's also offers many hamburgers, soups and sandwiches. Make sure you save room for dessert, including a rich chocolate fudge cake and cobbler of the day. You'll find 101 beers including a thirst quenching 52 on tap, plus fine wine and premium spirits. The tequila connoisseur will be equally pleased with 42 tequila varieties. You can sit outside, if you like, and get that much closer to the Sierra Nevada backdrop that inspires this restaurant. For classic western flavor bring the family and come join the friendly staff at Red's Old 395 Grill.

1055 S Carson Street, Carson City NV
(775) 887-0395

JT Basque Bar & Dining Room

The Victorian structure which houses the JT Basque Bar & Dining Room was moved to its present location in Gardnerville from the Virginia City area in 1896. The building has served as a saloon and dining hall throughout its more than 100 year history in downtown Gardnerville. In 1960, two immigrant Basque sheepherders, brothers Jean and Pete Lekumberry, and Jean's wife, Shirley, purchased the establishment. Jean and Shirley raised their three children, Robert, Marie Louise and J.B., here. Today, J.B., his family and Marie Louise are proud to continue a great dining tradition. The multi-course family-style meals hearken back to the boarding house origins of the dining hall. No menu and no questions—guests are greeted straight away by steaming tureens of soup and a bottle of burgundy table wine. Following the soup is a fresh green salad, lightly dressed in vinegar and oil. After the salad come hearty bowls of Basque beans and a stew that changes daily. The stew could be a simple lamb, beef or chicken and rice, or it might be the more exotic ox-tail or tongue, depending on the day of the week. Next comes your choice of one of the main entrées: succulent steak, lamb, Basque chicken or sweetbreads. Weekend specials might include a Basque-style scampi, grilled salmon or roasted rabbit. All entrées come with the JT's world famous homemade French fries. Rounding out the meal is ice cream and coffee. Most visitors to the JT begin with a stop at the bar for the traditional Basque apéritif known as Picon Punch. True to its name, this tasty libation packs a punch. The feeling inside the classic western saloon and dining hall is always fun and friendly with a convivial mix of locals and visitors sharing a good time. As one happy diner put it, "At the JT, it's a good time, every time."

1426 U.S. Highway 395, Gardnerville NV   (775) 782-2074

Barone and Reed Food Company

Located in the historic corridor of old Minden, the Barone and Reed Food Company was established in 2004. The property is the original site of owner Alan Reed's family business, Warren Reed Insurance, founded in 1947 by Alan's father, Warren. Over the years, the property served insurance and real estate customers of the Reed family and housed the first permanent library site in the Carson Valley. The Reed family invites you to visit their beautiful restaurant, designed by award-winning architect Niccolo Valerio of Beverly Hills. The restaurant features three dining sections, two bars and a private lounge (all kept warm and cozy by two large fireplaces) as well as the popular Chef's Table. While you're here, take a peek at the private wine room and then catch your breath as you gaze from the balcony at the Tuscan mural painted by San Diego artist Kathleen King. It's no wonder that one customer marveled, "Are we in San Francisco?" and another said, "This feels like Seattle or Napa." The ambience is similar, but you're at Barone and Reed Food Company in Minden, where the staff is eager to serve you and well-known Chef Christoph Waldburger stands ready to delight your palate. Barone and Reed Food Company—the one place you can't wait to visit, again and again.

1599 Esmeralda Avenue, Minden NV
(775) 783-1988

The Stone House Café

Located in an historic home built entirely from stone, The Stone House Café's charming façade hints at the warmth and superb food inside. Award-winning chef Paul Abowd and his late wife, Adele, built a huge reputation in Carson City with Adele's Restaurant & Lounge. Paul sold Adele's to his son, Charlie, in 1998. He opened The Stone House Café in 2005 with daughter and manager Cyrina Abowd. The Stone House provides great choices any time of day with extensive breakfast, lunch and dinner menus. Breakfast options include old-fashioned Banana Rum French Toast, *huevos rancheros* or the smoked salmon omelette. Sandwiches with Imagination highlight the lunch menu, along with wraps, burgers, soups and salads. The Stone House features an eclectic dinner menu that makes choosing pleasant. French onion soup is a popular starter. For a main course, try the chicken livers sautéed with shallots, garlic and wild forest mushrooms, the Lobster Savannah or the veal with scampi. Chef Paul enjoys the challenge of creating new dishes to keep the menu fresh and customers coming back. Come inside and enjoy inventive entrées and impeccable service or relax outside on the heated patio. Either way you'll enjoy memorable food by one of Nevada's most renowned chefs.

1907 S Arlington Avenue, Reno NV
(775) 284-3895
www.stonehousecafereno.com

Great Basin Brewing Co.

You can enjoy fresh, hand-crafted ales and lagers brewed right before your eyes at Great Basin Brewing Co., Nevada's oldest and most award-winning brewery-restaurant. Proprietors Tom and Bonda Young share a long-time passion for fine European-style beers. While Tom worked as a geologist he became hooked by sampling many wonderful beers in Europe. His passion grew as he studied brewing as a home-brewer at UC Davis and at numerous micro-breweries, prior to putting down roots in downtown Sparks in 1993. Great Basin brews four flagship styles available year-round and has six to 10 seasonal Brewmaster's Specials. The most popular brew is an aromatic, hoppy, American-style India pale ale named Ichthyosaur, after the official state fossil, which the locals affectionately refer to as Icky. This fortifying brew is fit to resurrect the giant fish-lizard that was once the king of seas during the Jurassic period. Great Basin boasts a great menu to complement the award-winning brews. Patrons rave about the hand-cut Wild Horse Ale battered fish and chips, the spicy Black and Blue Burger (so unique that the name is trademarked), char-broiled steaks and the legendary garlic fries. From salads to sausage sandwiches, the menu hits plenty of high notes that pair nicely with the brews. The atmosphere at Great Basin Brewing Co. is enhanced by wood floors and murals depicting the rugged beauty of the Great Basin. Check the website for the current beer selection and entertainment schedule.

846 Victorian Avenue (two blocks E of Nugget), Sparks NV
(775) 355-7711
www.greatbasinbrewingco.com

The Lodge at Galena

Just off the Mount Rose Highway, a stately wooden dwelling lies beneath the pine trees. This is the Lodge at Galena. A casually elegant restaurant, the Lodge offers exquisite panoramic views, an impressive wine and beer list and sumptuous food. Owners Eric and Corin Roth have created an enticing menu that offers something for every palate. Popular starters, which work equally well as pub snacks for those catching a game on the big screen, include coco-almond prawns and tangy Asian pot stickers. You can also choose salads, sandwiches and burgers, as well as succulent steaks, pasta and seafood dishes. Consider the Vodka Ravioli or the Lodge's signature Blue Moon fish platter. For dessert, you might try a traditional sweet or a sweet martini such as the Crème Brûlée or Ultimate Chocolate Raspberry. These delicious concoctions will make you happy you're an adult. The Roths purchased the Lodge in 2006 with the help of Corin's grandparents, Wayne and Nadine, who were delighted to help their grandkids fulfill their long-held dream of owning a restaurant. Enjoy a dining experience in a place where the wine meets the pine—the Lodge at Galena.

**17025 Mount Rose Highway, Reno NV
(775) 849-2100**

Napa-Sonoma Grocery Company

Napa-Sonoma Grocery Company in Reno understands the finer things in life and brings them to you in abundance. Gourmet food and beverages are at the heart of Napa-Sonoma offerings along with a selection of fine gifts for the kitchen. The gourmet food is available catered, in gift baskets or prepared at the in-store deli, where you can stop for lunch. You can also arrange for a private dinner in the store's spacious dining room. Owners Marty and Paula Kloska go the extra mile to meet their customers' desires. Their experienced chefs will customize catering for your event or bring hot lunches to your office to make that long meeting more bearable. Their gift shop features ready-made gift baskets or custom baskets filled with your choice of candy, gourmet grocery items, gifts and fine boutique wines, including the Napa-Sonoma brand. The store specializes in a selection of Nevada-produced groceries to give your baskets a local feel. Beyond gift baskets, look for name brand collectibles, a large selection of bath and body products, candles and baby gifts. Kitchen or wine accessories and Polish pottery are always a treat. The store provides a personal shopper service and a friendly staff to assist you with your gift giving needs. Napa-Sonoma pulls out the stops to offer you every accommodation, including a bridal registry, gift wrapping, delivery and shipping. For a gourmet shopping experience in a class by itself, visit Napa-Sonoma Grocery Company.

294 E Moana Lane, #10, Reno NV (775) 826-0595 *www.napa-sonoma.com*

Sport Haus

Sport Haus can handle every step of purchasing and maintaining your luxury vehicle or sports car. Owners John and Emilie McClure opened Sport Haus, an independent dealership, in 1980. Many of their customers have been with them since they opened, thanks to the selection of hard-to-find exotic cars, world class service and relaxed sales approach. Come visit Northern Nevada's largest indoor showroom where you can find everything from a late-model BMW sport utility vehicle to a vintage Porsche. General Sales Manager Mitch Berney says, "Feel free to come take a look at our incredible inventory of Mercedes, Audis, Jaguars, Porsches and other European and exotic cars. If you are not able to visit us in person, then check out our virtual showroom included on our website." The Sport Haus service department employs ASE certified and factory trained technicians to keep your vehicle in tip-top condition. For the employees at Sport Haus, working on Porsches and other fine European and exotic cars is a way of life. In fact, after hours you will find many of them building and racing their own Porsches and motorcycles. Sport Haus carries a large inventory of parts for luxury and sport autos. If what you need is not in stock, Sport Haus will gladly order it for you. Visit Sport Haus, one of the nation's largest independently owned dealerships, to find the exact vehicle you have been searching for or to maintain that special one you already enjoy. Remember, if you don't see it in the showroom, John, Emilie and their staff will search until they find the car of your dreams.

9732 S Virginia Street, Reno NV
(775) 329-1447 or (877) 720-1988
www.sporthausinc.com

La Petite Variety & Gifts

Owners Cecilia and Victor Ortiz showcase gifts from Peru and other South American countries at La Petite Variety & Gifts in Reno. The Ortizes opened the shop in 2005 with the aim of offering plenty of variety to satisfy a diverse clientele. The store's specialties include Peruvian silver jewelry. You will find wine glasses that can be personally engraved for the coming-of-age celebration known as a *quinceanera* or for a wedding. A handmade photo book for a new baby or a newly married couple is always a thoughtful purchase. For something sure to be one-of-a-kind, consider one of the handmade purses. A local jeweler offers necklaces through the shop. For the woman in your life, consider a fur wrap, scarves or hair combs. Men appreciate the belts, wallets, watches and money clips. You'll find many collectibles here along with such home décor items as decorator lamps, picture frames and candles. Top off your gift selection with a handmade card. La Petite also carries a line of gourmet soaps and body creams made of all natural herbs and fragrances by Claude Poissonniez, a native of Belgium. Competitive pricing and weekly discounts make La Petite a compelling choice. Communication is easy, because both English and Spanish are spoken here. When you are looking for something made by hand, consider the variety at La Petite Variety & Gifts.

900 Holman Way, Sparks NV
(775) 359-5558

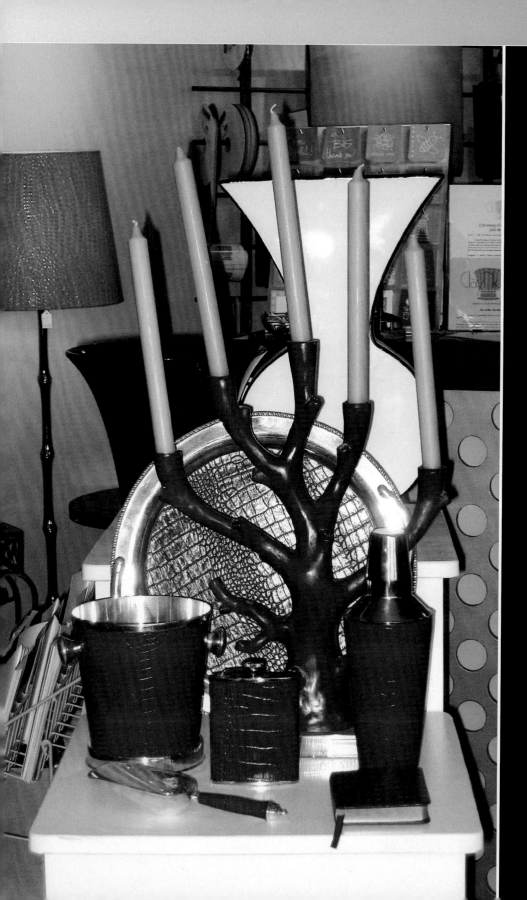

ClayNichols

What's part eclectic art gallery, part bookstore, part jewelry shop, and part gift store featuring furnishings and home accents? It's ClayNichols, a one-of-a-kind Reno store that mixes up styles and periods in fun and functional ways. Owners Jean Nichols and Jackie Clay opened this store in 2005, and put their varied backgrounds to good use here. Jackie, a former history museum curator and director, brings an eye for detail and style to every display in the store. Jean was an avid traveler before becoming a stay-at-home mom and community volunteer. Her talent for finding new purposes for antiques helps define the ClayNichols environment. The furnishings here, which include vintage lamps, tables, cabinets and bowls, complement more modern pieces. Gifts range from bold jewelry choices to candles. Fine art has a prominent place here, with works in nearly every medium. Whether you're looking for paintings, photos or sculptures, you'll find many pieces by local artists and special showings throughout the year. The store also is known for its selection of Nevada related books. Jean and Jackie place a premium on getting to know every customer. For a store that will stir your imagination and add pleasure to your day, visit ClayNichols.

106 California Avenue, Reno NV
(775) 324-0505
www.claynichols.com

Just Wrapped UP!

Are you looking for an artful way to put the finishing touches on a carefully chosen gift? At Just Wrapped UP!, Valerie and Paul Rios' gift wrap and accessories store, the vast selection of gift wrap, tissue paper, ribbons and bows provides everything needed for the perfect gift presentation. This one-of-a-kind gift-wrapping *paperia* offers more than 200 unique paper designs, including Asian silkscreen, handmade textured paper, embroidered papers, Japanese papers and designs by Frank Lloyd Wright. The shop can tuck special toppers and enhancements, such as beads, charms and miniature ornaments into bows for extra panache. Specialized gifts bags come in a plethora of shapes, sizes and themes to suit any gift. Just Wrapped UP! offers shoppers three options. They can purchase supplies for wrapping at home, take advantage of the store's gift-wrapping service or use the workstations to wrap the gift themselves in the store. Creative consultants can help with clever gift-wrapping solutions, gift baskets and bulk wrapping for personal or corporate clients. From tags to wine bags, it's all here. Whether you need an extra-large bow big enough for a car or house or paper personalized with your company name, logo or photo, stop in soon and discover all the exquisite options available at Just Wrapped UP!

3366 Lakeside Court, Reno NV
(775) 829-7174
www.justwrappedup.com

Michael & Son's

If you're looking for elegant and distinctive Southwest Native American art and fine jewelry, you'll find it at Michael & Son's in Reno. Five in-house jewelers create custom pieces using silver, gold and platinum as well as Nevada turquoise. Michael and Mary Lorenz started the business more than 20 years ago in a 400-square-foot shop. Today, a 2,000-square-foot facility offers full-service jewelry repair and design, plus a gift shop. The shop now belongs to Michael and Mary's son David and his wife, Shannon, who make customer satisfaction their goal. David, who attended the Revere Academy of Jewelry Arts in San Francisco, has a passion for jewelry and takes pride in creating custom pieces for his customers, from necklaces, rings, bracelets and earrings to custom wedding sets and mother's rings. He has even created jewelry for Pope John Paul II, Bill Cosby and Rita Coolidge. The shop carries Native American jewelry and art, including the largest selection of handmade Indian baskets in northern Nevada, pottery and dolls. You'll also find the official jewelry line of the University of Nevada Wolf Pack football team. David goes directly to the artists for all art pieces carried in the store. Whether you are searching for an artistic gift or a jewelry creation made especially for you, come by Michael & Son's.

2001 E 2nd Street, Reno NV
(775) 786-5110 or (800) 785-5110
www.michaelandsons.com

Paper Moon

Whimsical and colorful, Paper Moon looks and feels more like a boutique than a typical card store. The flower and pattern cards are so bright and cheery that you might be tempted to buy them by the hundreds and use them as wallpaper. Owner Laura Ganchan-Romero can understand such a reaction, though she suggests that you stick to using cards for their original purposes. Whether you need to express a simple thank you to a gracious host or to wish your big brother a happy birthday, you'll find plenty of choices at Paper Moon. If you haven't connected with that college friend in some time, you can make a style statement while you're at it by choosing a chic, plaid or retro card. Located in Plumgate, Paper Moon carries a huge selection of bulk paper and card stock as well. The lines of side items add to the hip atmosphere, particularly the handbags. Each style has a personality all its own, featuring name brands such as Vera Bradley, Nah and Little Earth. These bags go great with jeans and some would look right in place at an outdoor rock festival. Add Paper Moon to your list of cheerful shopping destinations in Reno.

550 W Plumb Lane, Suite E-1, Reno NV
(775) 827-9933

Best Wishes Cards & Gifts

Best Wishes Cards & Gifts has all the events of the year covered, from Valentine's Day to Christmas. The array of greeting cards and gifts changes with the season, complimenting the fine selection of home décor, ceramics and candles available year-round. Best Wishes is a dealer in popular collectibles such as Department 56, Fontanini from Roman, Christopher Radko, Lenox, Jim Shore's Heartwood Creek and Demdaco's Willow Tree figurines. A locally owned and operated Reno favorite since 1983, the store is located in the Franktown Corners Shopping Arcade, close to the airport. Best Wishes is a dependable source when you need just the right card to celebrate a special occasion or express yourself with congratulations, gratitude or sympathy. You can also select from the multitude of papers, stickers and rubber stamps to create the perfect page for your scrapbook or invitation for your next event. While you are shopping downstairs for your everyday needs, remember it's always Christmas upstairs in the Christmas Shoppe. There you will find a wonderland of Christmas decorations and ornaments, Department 56 villages and Fontanini nativity scenes. Owner Lee Baldock and store manager Barbara McHenry are proud to provide the most complete selection of these collectibles in Northern Nevada. Ask the staff what separates their shop from the chain stores and they will tell you, "We care about service." Whatever the occasion, Best Wishes Cards & Gifts awaits the opportunity to serve you.

2315 Kietzke Lane, Reno NV
(775) 825-1500
www.bestwishesreno.com

Photo by Nada Summers

Photo by Carol Vogel

Hoofbeats & Carriages

Is there a more romantic way to get to a wedding than in a beautiful carriage, drawn by a pale, majestic Norwegian Fjord horse? For more than 25 years, Carson City-based Hoofbeats & Carriages has been treating brides and grooms like royalty on their special day. Owner Steven Summers is well known to residents of these parts, along with his prized mare, Bella, who is constantly getting hugs from people on the street. Steven has many years of horse experience, dating back to his days in 4-H. He owns a fleet of carriages and a herd of horses ready to take you on a magical journey through Carson City and Reno. If you're looking for an elegant ride to a wedding or other special occasion, you'll thrill to a ride in one of the beautiful, old-style carriages. Steven also offers tours of the region, providing historical information and commentary. Those looking for a much more rustic experience can take a ride in an authentic covered wagon similar to those used to head west in the 1800s. Hoofbeats & Carriages uses champion Norwegian Fjord horses, known for their light-colored coats and the black stripe that runs from the top of their heads to the tip of their tails. The Fjords also possess the strength and gentle nature that makes them excellent draft animals. Take a historic tour of the wagon trains or arrive at your wedding, anniversary or birthday party in style with the services of Hoofbeats & Carriages.

2240 Bunch Way, Carson City NV
(775) 882-5533
www.horsedrawncarriages.net

Men Wielding Fire

In their 40-foot, mobile kitchen on wheels, Jack Lyons and Mike Sylvester have all the equipment and knowledge they need to cater a fancy gourmet fête or a good old-fashioned barbecue. Their Reno catering business, Men Wielding Fire, is getting a reputation throughout the U.S. as the place to call if you seek expert catering for a special occasion. They'll drive to weddings, big sporting events or family reunions to serve up a feast that's as elegant or as down-home as you wish it to be. They can even start your morning meeting with a full breakfast that includes their own freshly made pastries. Their entrées range from prime rib sandwiches and barbecued pork or chicken to grilled salmon and leg of lamb. They also offer a full slate of side dishes, salads and exquisite desserts. Men Wielding Fire just might be the greatest marriage between the discovery of fire and the invention of the wheel to come along. They have a separate trailer for their commercial rotisserie ovens and another with a full service bar, complete with 10 taps of your choice of micro and domestic beers. Whether you are entertaining 50 or 5,000, when you want hot, fresh food served on-site, call Jack and Mike at Men Wielding Fire.

Reno NV
(775) 786-1117 or (775) 691-9827
www.menwieldingfire.com

The Corley Ranch

Celebrating a birthday, family reunion or wedding on a working ranch is an opportunity to soak up both the Western spirit and the Western landscape. The Corley Ranch in scenic Carson Valley raises cattle and hay while accommodating parties as large as 500. The Sierra Nevada mountain range rises 10,000 feet on the horizon, and guests are close to Reno, Carson City and South Lake Tahoe. Eat or dance in an antique barn or outside under the stars. The Corley family can recommend caterers, Western musicians, cowboy poets or historic reenactments, such as a live shoot-out or fast-draw competition with Wyatt Earp or Buffalo Bill. You can enjoy wagon tours through the cattle and alfalfa fields. With luck, the hands may be branding cattle or putting up hay. Have a barbecue or taste grub prepared over an open fire and served from a chuck wagon. Take pleasure in the lawns and gardens. Play outdoor games such as volleyball and croquet or rally 'round a duck race, then roast marshmallows at an evening bonfire. The Harvest Festival takes place every weekend in October and features a two-acre corn maize, lots of activities, including pig races, and 18 varieties of pumpkins, winter squash, melons and more. Let Jon and Paula Corley and their daughter and son-in-law, Joni and John Roper, put a Western twist on your celebration at the Corley Ranch.

859 Highway 395 S, Gardnerville NV
(775) 265-3045
www.corleyranch.com

Sunset over Reno

Sunset over the Humboldt River, Winnemucca NV
Photo by Zach Sheppard

Greater Nevada

The Ruby Mountains
Photo by Jerry Gay

Quilts 4 Cancer

Barb Johnston, founder of Quilts 4 Cancer, knows firsthand what it's like to live with cancer. She is a survivor of breast cancer, and many members of her family have lived with and sometimes died of cancer. In 1986, she started Quilts 4 Cancer with her husband, Jim, in upstate New York. They moved to Pahrump in 1999. It is Barb's aim to give a handmade quilt to as many cancer patients as possible. Volunteers throughout the country create quilts for children. The organization has recently concentrated local efforts on quilts for adults undergoing cancer treatment in Nye County. "Being treated with chemotherapy makes you feel cold all the time," says Barb, yet warmth is not the key purpose in providing the quilts. "Just to know someone is thinking and caring about them is what we hope the cancer patients get from receiving the quilts," she says. She values the positive response she receives from cancer patients. Barb is always looking for new quilters as well as donations of money and fabric. A $30 donation is enough to create one adult-size quilt. Like many quilters, Barb finds quilting a relaxing hobby. Reach out and help Quilts 4 Cancer wrap cancer patients in serviceable handmade quilts crafted with love.

Pahrump NV
(775) 751-5356
www.quilts4cancer.org

Red Lion Inn & Casino

Red Lion Inn & Casino offers first-rate accommodations, family-friendly dining and exciting gaming. Soundproof rooms and comfortable, oversized beds promise a dreamy night's sleep, while coffee makers, hairdryers and available laundry service are always appreciated. The Inn can handle your business meeting or family needs with ease, thanks to 105 rooms and six family suites as well as facilities and catering services for meetings, conferences or special events. The Garden restaurant never closes and serves everything from ham and eggs to steak and lobster in a relaxed atmosphere. Dinner specials may include such favorites as lobster ravioli or roasted quail with cranberry Burgundy sauce. The Red Lion offers wireless Internet throughout, and corporate travelers will appreciate the computer, copier and fax provided in the business center. Other attractions include a seasonal heated outdoor pool, a video arcade and a newly opened fitness center equipped with treadmills and stationary bicycles. Watch your favorite teams on one of the four high-definition big-screen televisions in the Sports Bar, or perhaps play some video poker while relaxing with your favorite malt beverage. The Red Lion's intimate casino action features state-of-the-art slot machines, blackjack and three card poker. Whether you are planning an overnight stay, a weekend getaway or an evening out with family and friends, include the Red Lion Inn & Casino in your plans.

741 W Winnemucca Boulevard, Winnemucca NV (775) 623-2565 *www.redlionwinn.com*

Country Hearth Inns & Suites

Country Hearth Inns & Suites offers guests old-fashioned hospitality, large accommodations and a friendly and efficient staff. All 109 rooms at the Elko inn feature refrigerators, cable television with premium channels, coffeemakers and alarm clocks. Guest laundry facilities make the inn as ideal for extended stay guests as it is for overnighters. Country Hearth offers a mix of lodgings, including luxurious bridal Jacuzzi suites and comfortable family suites. General Manager Sara Ball and Front Desk Manager Serena Simler enjoy people, and their attitude shows in the hotel's warm and welcoming ambience. Country Hearth features the InnCredible Breakfast, a large breakfast buffet, every morning. The menu changes daily, but often includes biscuits and gravy, scones and omelettes. Around 5 pm, expect to see coffee, tea, milk and generously sized cookies laid out for guests to enjoy. In addition, the 24-hour indoor pool, spa and fitness center make it easy for guests to adhere to exercise regimens while traveling or to simply relax at the end of the day. Country Hearth is conveniently located close to casinos, the Northeastern Nevada Museum and shopping. Your stay will be as close to home as the staff can make it at Country Hearth. For all the charm of a bed and breakfast and all the conveniences of a hotel, make your reservations at Country Hearth Inns & Suites.

1930 Idaho Street, Elko NV
(775) 738-8787 or (800) 600-6001
www.countryhearth.com

71 Ranch

Looking for an authentic ranch adventure where you really can ride the open range? Experience the West the old fashioned way, from the back of a horse. The 71 Ranch is a real cattle ranch, right in the middle of cowboy country near Elko, that offers guests the chance to be part of day-to-day ranch life for an authentic working-cowboy experience. Discover the other Nevada—vast meadows, endless sagebrush prairies, rolling foothills and rugged mountain trails. You can ride all day on the more than 38,000 privately deeded acres and still not cover a fraction of the country. You will have the chance to push a few cows (the ranch runs about 3,000 head of cattle) or for a more laid-back adventure, enjoy hay rides, outdoor cookouts and stories around the campfire. Wildlife is abundant on the ranch. Deer and antelope often cross your trail while eagles and red tailed hawks soar overhead. Weekly ranch vacation packages available from April through October include comfortable accommodations in the historic 71 Ranch lodge or in cozy individual cabins. Hearty, ranch-style meals are prepared by the 71's master chef. Enjoy delicious homemade dishes that feature the 71's own ranch-raised beef. The staff takes its commitment to each guest seriously and offers genuine western hospitality. The 71 Ranch also provides a comfortable setting for corporate retreats or family reunions, and during the winter season overnight lodging and a hearty breakfast are available when you sign up for the 71 Ranch Bunk & Breakfast plan. Take scenic trail rides, drive cattle, learn to throw a rope and ride to your heart's content. Explore the real American West and make memories that last a lifetime at the 71 Ranch.

State Road 229, Deeth NV
(775) 753-6745 or (866) 717-7171
www.71-ranch.com

Fallon Comfort Inn

Are you looking for clean, comfortable lodging that feels like a home away from home? The Fallon Comfort Inn features 82 newly refurbished rooms that offer a welcoming yet restful atmosphere. Some accommodations boast whirlpool tubs as well, and others are pet-friendly. Corporate and vacationing travelers will appreciate the business center and wireless high-speed Internet. Guests can work up a sweat in the fitness center or relax in the indoor pool and hot tub. Situated in an ideal location between Great Basin National Park and Las Vegas, the inn is a mere 45 minutes from Virginia City, a town rich in gold mining history and only an hour away from both Carson City, the state capital, and the gaming paradise of Reno. Just minutes away, Sand Mountain provides a playground for ATVs, dune buggies, hikers and sand skiers. Fallon, which is part of the historic Pony Express Trail, is also the home of TOPGUN, the Navy Fighter Weapons School. Inn keepers Pranav and Divya Morar and their accommodating staff make 100 percent customer satisfaction their goal and have a long list of repeat customers to their credit. Three local churches house their visitors at the inn, and community groups gather at the inn's pool as well. Members of the National Hot Rod Association return every year as do Silver State rodeo groups. Come to the Fallon Comfort Inn and see why *comfort* is the most important part of its name.

1830 W Williams Avenue, Fallon NV
(775) 423-554 or (888) 691-6388
www.comfortinnfallon.com

Photo by Paulie Alles

Churchill County Museum & Archives

Photo by Cindy Loper

The Churchill County Museum & Archives brings history to life with artifacts, photographs and documents that illustrate the stories of humans and nature in Churchill County. The museum's artifact collection, containing more than 19,000 items, includes period clothing and accessories, textiles, quilts, and kitchen and household accessories. The equipment of various professions, such as a doctor's buggy, a steam-powered tractor and a blacksmith shop with tools, enable visitors to grasp the reality of life in the county's early days. Other reminders of daily life include a restored Red Crown gasoline pump, local school bells and the inevitable outhouse. The Woodliff Novelty Store, one of the oldest buildings in Fallon, was moved to the museum and opened to the public in 1984 following restoration. In addition to artifacts, the museum's photographic collection alone contains 40,000 photographs. These photos have been catalogued in a computer database, making them easy to use for research and exhibit purposes, and copies of most of them are available for purchase. The Churchill County Museum also holds some City of Fallon and Churchill County records in its archive. Special speakers, children's events, and Museum Association newsletters enlighten local folks by explaining the past. Take some time today to tour the Churchill County Museum. From vintage wedding dresses to Indian artifacts, you're sure to find something fascinating here.

1050 S Maine Street, Fallon NV
(775) 423-3677
www.ccmuseum.org

City of Fallon

Born during the California Gold Rush, Fallon combines old-time agrarian culture with the 21st century's cutting edge. During the western migration, travelers stopped along the Carson River to rest after crossing the treacherous 40-Mile Desert. The settlement was called Ragtown, named for the clothes and blankets that could be seen drying on trees, fence posts and wagon wheels. Modern-day Fallon is just six miles east of that original resting spot. At the turn of the 20th century the first federal reclamation project in the United States, the Newlands Project, was created. It diverted water from the Carson and Truckee Rivers to reclaim the desert for ranches and farms around Fallon, helping settle the west. The area's most famous crop is the Hearts of Gold cantaloupe that was shipped nationwide in the 1920s and today lends its name to the annual Labor Day festival. Fallon is also home to Naval Air Station Fallon, which is home to the Naval Fighter Weapons School, code-named TOPGUN, made famous by the movie starring Tom Cruise. The Lahontan Valley wetlands surround Fallon and provide outstanding bird watching in the spring and waterfowl hunting in the fall. There is a lot to see and do in Fallon and visitors are always treated with good ol' fashioned hospitality. If you look to the sky, you just might see pilots with nerves of steel flying over fields of Hearts of Gold when you visit the city of Fallon.

**100 Campus Way, Fallon NV
(Convention Center)**
(775) 423-4556
www.fallontourism.com

Tonopah Historic Mining Park

The Tonopah Historic Mining Park brings history to life with exhibits of mining artifacts on the site and in the original buildings. The park encompasses more than 100 acres and is located on Jim and Belle Butler's original claim that started the silver rush to Tonopah in 1900. Many of the mining and processing techniques developed then are still utilized today. The park's main attraction, the Burro Tunnel Underground Adventure, features a self-guided walking tour down a mine tunnel that culminates in visitors stepping into a steel viewing cage that is suspended over the 500-foot vertical excavation. The newly restored Mizpah Mine collar allows visitors to walk across the top of the richest mine in the Tonopah District and look down the lighted shaft. Current displays and equipment include three head frames and hoists, an original ore-sorting grizzly, an ore crusher, roller mill and extensive mineral displays that include a black light mineral exhibit. All buildings in the park are open to allow visitors to visualize how it felt to be working in a turn of the century mining environment. In 2006, *Nevada Magazine's* Best of Nevada Readers' Awards named the Tonopah Historic Mining Park the Best Museum in Rural Nevada for the fifth straight year. Come explore the Queen of the Silver Camps for yourself and experience a rich chapter in Nevada's history.

520 McCulloch Avenue, Tonopah NV
(775) 482-9274
www.tonopahnevada.com

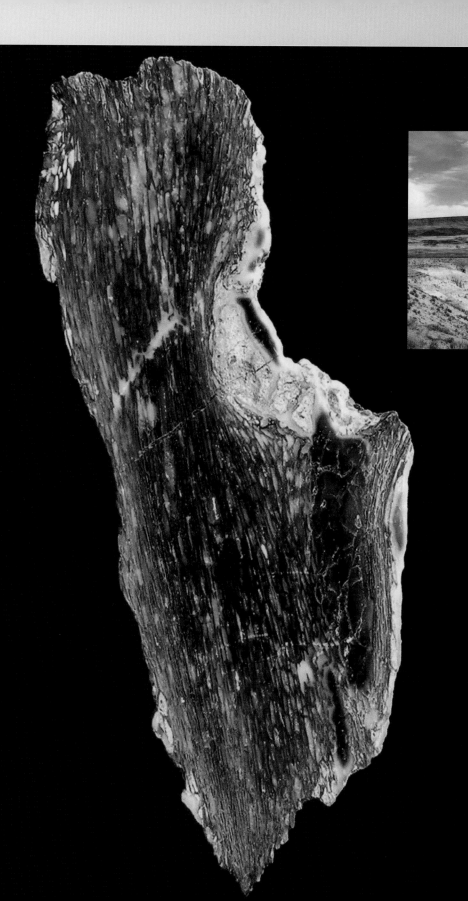

Royal Peacock Opal Mines

The Royal Peacock Opal Mines are in the Virgin Valley, a region renowned for stunning fire opals including the spectacular black opal, which is the Nevada state precious gemstone. The action of volcanically super-heated water on silicon-rich ash layers formed these gems more than 14 million years ago. The most spectacular examples of the opals are on permanent display in the Smithsonian Institution in Washington D.C. Today, visitors can dig their own gems at the Royal Peacock Opal Mines. Anything they unearth is theirs to keep. Owners Harry and Joy Wilson and family members Walter Wilson, Angie Estes and Julie Key also run a rock shop where enthusiasts can purchase exquisite fluorescent and moss opals and other mineral specimens. Looking for more than a day trip? Royal Peacock offers full RV hookups and spaces for tent campers. A laundry helps erase the traces of dusty mining adventures, and campers can pick up groceries and supplies in nearby Denio, right on the Oregon border. The beautiful high desert also offers mule deer and antelope hunting in season as well as fishing in several stocked ponds. Hiking the canyons may yield a fossil find or two and maybe even glimpses of desert creatures such as burros and waterfowl. Or how about a relaxing soak in a hot springs pool? The mine is open from May 15 through October 15, weather permitting. Come have an adventure you'll remember at the Royal Peacock Opal Mines.

Denio NV
(775) 941-0374 (mine)
(775) 272-3246 (phone in winter)
www.royalpeacock.com

Lattin Farms

The motto at Lattin Farms is We Grow Food and Family Fun. With the huge variety of activities and things to eat here, it's easy to see why. This land, in the Lahontan Valley, has been in the Lattin family since 1908. Current owners Rick and B Ann Lattin are the fifth generation to own and operate the farm, but the first generation to open it up as an attraction. Rick and B Ann started the transformation of the farm with a little stand that offered melons, raspberries and tomatoes from the farm, plus breads, jellies and pickles. Business exploded, and the Lattins began adding more attractions. One of the most famous of them is the Nevada Maze, cut into a cornfield more than four acres wide, which attracts more than 25,000 visitors a year looking for the exit. The puzzle changes every year. A Critterville petting zoo lets children of all ages feed and interact with goats, rabbits and turkeys. An antique tour exhibits farming implements from years gone by. Finally, nothing says family farm like a good, old-fashioned hayride. You can also pick your own produce. These activities, and many others, guarantee fun for families. Lattin Farms also caters and is available for weddings and special parties. If you're looking for great food and a good time, come to Lattin Farms.

1955 McLain Road, Fallon NV (775) 867-3750 *www.lattinfarms.com*

Ely Renaissance Society

After years of boom or bust, the community of Ely saw the need for a diversified economy based on more than mining. Since 1999, the Ely Renaissance Society has sought to create an attractive downtown district filled with art and culture. The society was founded a month after the town's largest mine closed—the loss of 400 jobs underscored the need for new attractions. Today, visitors can wind through an 11-block outdoor cultural art gallery. The White Pine Public Museum with its 4th of July mural makes a good starting place for an art trail that leads to more than 20 art pieces, plus signs describing Ely's history. Various artists created large murals on local stores. These graphics depict the places and events that shaped Ely. You can walk by paintings of a cattle drive, a blacksmith's shop, a mine, a Shoshone woman gathering pine nuts and a Basque sheepherder watching over his flock. Along the way, visitors enjoy a sculpture garden with a labyrinth, a retro gas station, a courthouse filled with historic photos and two working soda fountains. You'll also find restaurants, gaming facilities and Wild West bars. Ely Renaissance Society invites you to visit the place Where the World Met and Became One.

591 Campton Street, Ely NV
(775) 289-8769
www.elyrenaissance.com

Brews Brothers Coffee

According to Bert and Sue Fox, proprietors of Brews Brothers Coffee, they aren't in the coffee business per se; they are in the business of making people happy. The Foxes, along with their two sons, Casey and Jesse, opened the popular coffee shop in 2001, as a part-time post-retirement project. Brews Brothers Coffee offers a full selection of quality, espresso-based drinks, along with an array of tasty, freshly baked goods, including chocolate covered espresso beans and several flavors of flaky scones. Sue, a retired teacher who loves to read and share books, has turned a part of the eatery into a reading room and book exchange, where you can trade in a book you have already read for something new to read. Brews Brothers Coffee also offers a computer station for public use and wireless Internet access for those with laptops, which makes the coffee shop an ideal spot to gather with friends and colleagues. Bert and Sue pride themselves on their friendly service and are dedicated to providing a cozy respite for the community's busy denizens. Savor a great cup of coffee, find a new book and make some new friends with a visit to Brews Brothers Coffee.

**1860 Idaho Street, Elko NV
(775) 738-2767**

Nature's Corner Health and Vitamin Shoppe

Nature's Corner is dedicated to your overall health and wellness and offers a wide selection of natural products, vitamins and supplements designed to keep you fit as a fiddle. The full-service shop is owned and operated by area businesswoman Katinka Nanna, a Netherlands native who has extensive knowledge about the products she carries and is always happy to help you find what you need. Katinka is also featured on a local weekly radio program where she promotes natural health and offers useful, logical advice on a myriad of subjects. Nature's Corner has an on-site ice cream counter where you can enjoy a scoop of ice cream, fresh fruit smoothies and bowls of crunchy soy nuts. The shop also has shelves lined with vitamins, nutrients and protein powders, as well as an array of skin care products. Katinka has started a secondary business just across the street called Artemis Boutique, where her healthy clientele can outfit themselves in style with an array of upscale clothing and fashion accessories. Katinka, Donna and Erin are dedicated to helping you achieve all of your health and wellness goals through diet aids, homeopathy, aromatherapy and other natural methods. Get in touch with the healthy inner you at Nature's Corner, which makes your health its primary concern.

330 W Winnemucca Boulevard, Winnemucca NV (775) 625-4330

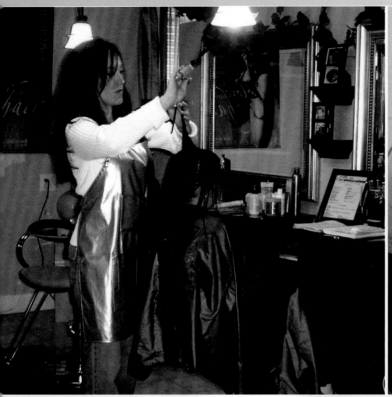

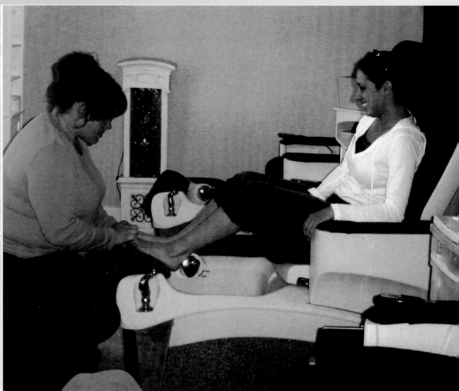

Bellissima Salon & Day Spa

After working with her parents in their hair salon for a couple of years, Angela Larramendy knew she wanted to pursue the same line of work. She also felt that Fallon needed a day spa that offered hair and nail services and rejuvenating spa treatments in one place. With the help of her husband, Gary, and a lot of sweat equity from her staff and their families, Bellissima Salon & Day Spa opened in June 2006. The 3,000-square-foot facility houses a pedicure room, an infrared sauna, a massage therapy room and an aesthetician's room, along with hair styling chairs and nail technician stations. Bellissima, which means beautiful you in Italian, offers hair, skin and nail services individually or as part of a package. Hair care options include cuts, colors, spiral perms and more for men, women and children. Bellissima is the only salon in Fallon that carries Bumble & Bumble of New York, Sexy Hair and Dermalogica hair care products. The salon also offers a variety of skin care services, from tinting treatments to wax treatments for everything from bikini lines to eyebrows. For the ultimate in relaxation and rejuvenation, clients may choose from six different types of massage therapy, including Swedish, sport and deep tissue. Spa packages offer popular combinations of services. Come refresh body and spirit at Bellissima Salon and Day Spa.

355 W First Street, Fallon NV (775) 428-1000

Workman Farms Crafts & Nursery

Whether you've got a gardener's green thumb, a quilter's nimble fingers or a taste for fresh produce, there's something for you at Workman Farms Crafts & Nursery. Owned by the Workman family for the past 45 years, this Fallon farm offers a variety of produce from January through October each year. The standout produce is Fallon's most famous culinary export, the Heart O' Gold cantaloupe. This sweet, juicy melon was first developed in the 1920s and soon became a national sensation. You'll also find a full array of fresh vegetables, great for cooking or crunching raw. With a full supply of seeds, shrubs and trees, annuals and perennials, Workman Farms can satisfy all of your gardening needs. Keep your plants healthy and attractive with the array of gardening supplies and treatments available at the nursery. Add that special decorative touch with a fountain or garden statue. Quilters will delight in the range of supplies at Workman Farms. You'll find a large variety of fabrics in many patterns. Workman Farms also stocks many cross-stitch and embroidery supplies and stencils. Rubber stamps, rug hooking and candle-making supplies are also available, as are pickling supplies, olives and spices. Whether you're looking for succulent melons, gear for your garden or crafting supplies, come to Workman Farms Crafts & Nursery.

4990 Reno Highway, Fallon NV
(775) 867-3716

Mountain Falls Golf Club

The firm of William Lyon Homes has built a master planned 950-acre golf community in Pahrump, and at the center of the community is the Mountain Falls Golf Club. "We want people to see that Mountain Falls is a real treasure," says a staff member. "The course is like an oasis." One-on-one service that you would expect in a small town is a club trademark. The club offers a top-notch golf course with reasonable rates and varying levels of challenge, from a course that plays at 5,415 yards from the ladies tees to a challenging 7,082-yard course from the men's championship tees. The course blends links and traditional golf course design. The front nine, designed by the Nicklaus design group, offers a links-style course that takes full advantage of the desert landscape. The back nine, designed by Cal Olson, offers traditional target-style play and use of landscaping, trees and water features. The clubhouse looks out at the 18th hole with imposing Mount Charleston in the background. It has a banquet area, a grill room and a lounge, as well as a fitness area with pools and workout machines. For those who live in the planned community taking shape around the golf course, lush landscapes continue into quiet neighborhoods with Tuscan-style homes, shaded paths and safe playgrounds. William Lyon Homes invites you to sample a southern Nevada lifestyle "where the grass is always greener, the stars are a little brighter and the future is filled with endless possibilities."

5001 Fox Avenue, Pahrump NV
(775) 537-6553
www.mountainfalls.com

Total Fitness Athletic Club, Inc.

Are you ready to accept the challenge of getting in shape and staying there? If so, you must visit Total Fitness Athletic Club (TFAC). Founder and co-owner Wayne Oceguera got his start in the fitness industry when he began lifting weights as a result of his training in Shudonkan Karate. Wayne holds a full-time job as a plumber in addition to working hard at the club in the evenings and on the weekends, keeping everything running smoothly. Wayne oversees the pro shop and keeps the equipment in top shape, while his wife, Angie, is the accounts manager. Wayne started the business with his partner, Lisa. You won't find a more inspirational role model than founder and co-owner Lisa Gough. Lisa lost her right leg below the knee when she was six as the result of a birth defect and she lost the rest of her leg above the knee in July 2002. After marrying young, she found herself a divorced and overweight mother of two. She decided to transform her body through bodybuilding. Now remarried, her unbreakably positive attitude is fueled by the support of her loving husband, Theron, and children Jeff and Jeremy. Lisa has gained many bodybuilding awards, including two first place trophies. Voted Fallon's Best Fitness Center in 2006 and 2007 in a local poll, TFAC features machines and free weights for toning and strength training, group fitness classes, childcare, a private woman's workout room, personal training and massage therapy. Visit this award-winning fitness center and let Wayne, Lisa and the team at TFAC inspire you to achieve peak fitness.

1925 W Williams Avenue, Fallon NV
(775)-428-BODY (2639)
www.tfacinc.com

Restaurante San Fermin

Southwest of France and tucked in between Cantabria and Navarra lies Spain's Basque Country, which over the centuries has created its own unique culture, complete with music, folklore and food. When Basque shepherds came to the Winnemucca area, their traditions became part of the fabric of Nevada's Great Basin and live on in such restaurants as Restaurante San Fermin. The popular eatery is owned and operated by Alicia Garijo and Jesus Flamarique, who are also the proprietors of another local favorite, Las Margaritas, which serves traditional Mexican foods and exceptional margaritas. Restaurante San Fermin offers a full menu of beef and seafood dishes as well as flavorful pastas and mouthwatering desserts. The upscale eatery boasts an atmosphere of casual fine dining, which makes it the ideal spot for a romantic dinner or a lunch with colleagues. The adjoining bar is decked out with a warm and welcoming wood interior and comfortable furniture, making it the perfect place to enjoy a cocktail in the company of good friends. Experience the sights, sounds and flavors of Basque Country right in the heart of Winnemucca at Restaurante San Fermin.

485 W Winnemucca Boulevard, Winnemucca NV (775) 625-4900

Sandwinds Restaurant & Sports Bar

For top-notch sports entertainment and seriously delicious steaks and seafood, come catch the action at the Sandwinds Restaurant & Sports Bar. Owner Larry F. Miller and his son, Kyle, vice-president of operations, provide plenty of lively entertainment to make folks feel at home and keep them coming back. Wednesday night is karaoke night. On Friday and Saturday nights, a partition wall opens up to transform part of the restaurant into a stage and large dance floor, featuring a DJ for dancing. Try the restaurant's signature Surf & Turf, a sizzling eight-ounce New York petite steak and succulent grilled shrimp paired with a baked potato and sautéed vegetables. Shrimp scampi and prime rib remain popular as well. The sports bar area features a full bar, pool table and big screen televisions, as well as Fox Sports' NFL promo package and promotional offers for tickets to shows in nearby Reno. Former President Jimmy Carter and his son, Democratic senatorial candidate Jack Carter, recently put Sandwinds on the map by stopping in at the restaurant after a campaign speech at the local VFW. When you want food, drink, sports and entertainment, check out the scene at the Sandwinds Restaurant & Sports Bar.

1120 Taylor Place, Fallon NV
(775) 423-8559

Partners in Wine

Winnemucca just cozied up that much closer to the western Pyrenees with the opening of Partners in Wine, a Basque market and eatery. The business celebrates the Basque culture with gifts, foodstuffs, wine and prepared cuisine from the Basque countryside that spans the mountains between France and Spain. Owners Vicki Gabiola and Andrea Goyhenetche prepare you for a Basque experience with dining tables covered with provincial cloths and wonderful aromas wafting from the kitchen. Partners in Wine specializes in what Vicki and Andrea call "twisted Basque" cuisine, which translates to Old World recipes brought into the 21st century through creative cooking. Luncheon fare includes the marinated pork known as *solomo*, a Basque steak or the Pyrenees Pollo sandwich. Vicki's Paella, the specialty of the house, combines a generous portion of chicken and chorizo paella with a crispy side salad and a freshly baked baguette. The appetizers are equally inspired and include classic *croquetas* as well as an array of cheese, fruit, mushrooms and olives. The milk products of the Basque countryside are celebrated with such desserts as flan or the delightfully sweet *arroz con leche*. A meal here could well inspire further exploration of Basque delicacies, and you will find a generous supply of these, including many wines, to take home. Discover the Basque side of Winnemucca at Partners in Wine.

1038 Grass Valley Road, Suite C, Winnemucca NV
(775) 623-9000

Dini's Lucky Club

Dini's Lucky Club is the oldest continuously family-operated casino in Nevada. The sprawling establishment offers two restaurants, Dini's Coffee Shop and Giuseppe's Steak House, plus the Cellar, a bar and lounge. Dini's is a place for locals to dine and dance, as well as tourists. First-time visitors are often struck by the cheerful attitude inside the casino, which at last count boasted 182 gaming machines. People playing the machines talk to each other, friends wave from across the room and anyone you pass seems to be smiling. At the Coffee Shop, the familiar food includes a legendary spaghetti buffet. Giuseppe's Steak House provides a fine dining experience and an extensive wine list in an atmosphere of casual elegance. The Cellar is a hopping place where live bands entertain customers on the weekends. Dini's has been a part of Yerington life since 1933, when Guiseppe "Joe" Dini, an Italian immigrant, opened a small bar and casino. He was soon able to move to a larger building and open Joe Dini's Lucky Club. Dini's has stayed in the family to this day. It still serves a roast beef sandwich special when the anniversary rolls around in October. That's in honor of Joe's wife, Elvira, who in the early days would cook up a roast on the weekends and fix sandwiches for customers. Joe's son, former Nevada Assembly Speaker Joe Dini, Jr., now owns Dini's. Jay and George, the sons of Joe, Jr., run the business. Fourth generation members of the family are now working at Dini's. You'll become a part of Yerington tradition when you visit Dini's Lucky Club.

45 N Main Street, Yerington NV
(775) 463-2868
www.dinisluckyclub.net

Stage Stop Café

Located in the Tonopah Station Ramada Inn, the Stage Stop Café features family-friendly dining and some of the best food in town. Owners Mathew and Bobei Misener, originally from Medford, Oregon, took over management of the restaurant from Mathew's uncle in 2003. Mathew's grandmother's grandmother, Sara Earp, lived in Tonopah and was the sister of Western legend Wyatt Earp. The Stage Stop Café serves breakfast, lunch and dinner, and marks house specialties on its menu with the sign of a horseshoe. Breakfast, served anytime, includes pancakes, waffles and eggs with ham, bacon or sausage. Heartier appetites will welcome any of the skillets or three-egg omelettes, such as the Country Omelette, a house specialty stuffed with sausage, bacon, bell peppers and onions, and topped with creamy country gravy. Try one of the many versions of quarter-pound hamburgers for lunch or enjoy the signature Hawaiian Melt, made with ham, pineapple and cream cheese on grilled sourdough. Dinner options include steaks, chicken dishes, fish and seafood, with soups, salads and an assortment of appetizers and desserts rounding out the menu. Stage Stop offers a kid's menu for all three meals, seating for nonsmokers and healthful low-cal plates for those who are watching their waistlines. Just steps away from the Ramada Inn and casino, tour buses stop at the café for lunch. For wonderfully fresh food and a taste of the Old West, stop at Stage Stop Café.

1137 S Main Street, Tonopah NV
(775) 482-8502

Flying Pig Bar-B-Q

A local favorite for more than 14 years, Flying Pig Bar-B-Q dishes up surprising variety in a casual, fun-filled atmosphere. Well known for fantastic barbecue, Flying Pig offers tender pulled pork sandwiches, habit-forming chicken wings and ribs worth a special trip to Winnemucca. Flying Pig reaches well beyond barbecue with such selections as tri-tip sandwiches, chicken or shrimp pesto pasta. The restaurant offers take-out as well as a fun and friendly environment for those who choose to dine in. Mike Jenkins, who purchased the business four years ago, continues to maintain the standards and reputation of the Flying Pig while focusing on ways to make everything even better. Executive Chef Ernensto Villagomez oversees all kitchen activities, as he has for the past 10 years, to ensure that every menu item that leaves the kitchen is top flight. Flying Pig also offers a lounge where locals often meet up with their friends to watch a game. You will find plenty to amuse you the Flying Pig. Try your luck at the slot machines, challenge your buddies to a game of darts, or enjoy a hotly contested round of foosball. For consistently great barbecue and a sports pub atmosphere, head on down to Flying Pig Bar-B-Q.

1100 W Winnemucca Boulevard, Winnemucca NV
(775) 623-4104

Symphony's at the Winery

Visitors to the Pahrump Valley Winery enjoy tours of Nevada's oldest and largest winery, but there is even more pleasure available at Symphony's at the Winery, the on-site restaurant. Open for lunch and dinner, the restaurant offers some of Nevada's finest food, beautifully served in an atmosphere of quiet elegance, at reasonable prices and with a sensible casual dress code. A warm and intimate dining room offers views of the beautifully landscaped grounds, the vineyard and Mount Charleston. The cuisine is new American and uses only the freshest and finest ingredients. For an entrée, try the filet mignon or the line-caught halibut from the deep waters of Alaska. Perhaps the restaurant's most famous dish is the signature Winery Scampi, shrimp sautéed in the award-winning Symphony wine that gives the restaurant its name. (This smooth, semi-sweet white has similarities to Riesling.) The quality of the cuisine, the superb service and serene ambience of the dining room have resulted in rave reviews by food critics and travel writers countrywide. *Zagat* has named it Pahrump's best dining experience three years in a row. The real tributes, however, come from the many Pahrump and Las Vegas regulars, who return to dine at the winery again and again. Locals consider it *the* place to come for special occasions such as birthdays or anniversaries. Reservations are highly recommended. Three helicopter pads are available for visits by the rich and famous. For a truly memorable meal, schedule a trip to Symphony's at the Winery.

3810 Winery Road, Pahrump NV (775) 751-7800 or (800) 368-9463
www.pahrumpwinery.com

Ormachea's Dinner House

Ormachea's Dinner House serves generous portions of hearty Basque fare in a warm and welcoming environment. The restaurant's fireplace, mellow wood furniture and the incredible aromas coming from the kitchen create a homelike atmosphere the moment you step inside. When Steve Patterson learned that his company was downsizing, he and his wife, Honorine, returned home to Winnemucca and opened Ormachea's in 1995. Chef Honorine stirs up her Basque family recipes from scratch with skill and love. Traditional specialties include Basque meatballs, Basque chicken baked in a salsa and *solomo*, which is thinly sliced aged and seasoned pork loin grilled with sautéed pimento. Unlike old-school Basque restaurants that serve meals family-style at long tables, Ormachea's offers restaurant-style service at smaller, more intimate tables. Ormachea's features a variety of entrées, including fresh seafood, pork, lamb chops and juicy steaks that are consistently a cut above the rest. An array of appetizers and nightly homemade desserts complete the menu. While you're there, be sure to sample picon punch, the Basque national drink. Stop in and discover for yourself why folks drive from miles around to have dinner at Ormachea's Dinner House.

180 Melarkey Street, Winnemucca NV (775) 623-3455

Buffmott's Antiques & Eweniques

While many folks consider retirement to be a time for relaxation, travel or puttering in the garden, Ted and Sharon Doke decided it was the perfect time to pursue their passion for antiques and collectibles. The spry couple put their lifelong love of fine antiques and bits of Americana to work for them when they opened Buffmott's Antiques & Eweniques, a charming collectibles business located just off of Elko's main drag, Idaho Street. Throughout the shop the couple's adorable ewe motif greets visitors and brings a smile to the faces of shoppers young and old. This welcoming shop resides in a beautifully maintained older home and offers a full spectrum of one-of-a-kind antique delights, including pottery, glassware, furniture, and Western memorabilia and collectibles. Ted and Sharon have created a monument to controlled chaos by carefully arranging a plethora of goods into chic vignettes that allow for easy shopping and hours of joyful browsing. Although the duo adore their antiques, they are also thrilled with the service side of their business and are always happy to take time out to visit with guests, crack a few jokes and help you find the perfect piece for your home or collection. Find original pieces of history and make some new friends with a stop at Buffmott's Antiques & Eweniques.

500 5th Street, Elko NV
(775) 738-7367

Smoke Signals
Trading Post & Gallery

Visitors to Ely find a memorable experience waiting for them at Smoke Signals Trading Post & Gallery. The 20-year-old business belongs to its founders, Laura Rainey-Carpenter and Fred Carpenter. The shop is part store and part museum, and has artifacts that date back thousands of years, such as a 12,000-year-old bison skull. Laura is a silversmith from the Western Shoshone tribe. Her work is displayed amidst the Native American jewelry, baskets and pottery that decorate the walls and cases of the shop. You can listen to the soft melody of a flute while browsing through these Indian treasures, as well as products from local Nevada craftspeople. Items of interest include antler carvings, knives of obsidian and antler, pen and ink drawings, clothing and tools. Children can stay occupied for hours with the games at Smoke Signals, and crafters delight in patterns for hide clothing and other specialty products. Laura can explain the significance of the bundles of sage and incense and tell captivating stories about items in the shop. Immerse yourself in arts and crafts that are as striking as the Western landscape that inspired them. Pay a visit to Smoke Signals Trading Post & Gallery.

598 Aultman Street, Ely NV
(775) 289-4848 or (800) 546-1151

Goodnight Irene

Shopping at Goodnight Irene could end up being as enjoyable a gift shopping experience as the classic folk song that gave this Winnemucca business its name. Rosita Kottke and daughter Katie Dockter opened the eclectic gift boutique in 2004 with the help of daughters Elaine Roth and Irene Kottke. Katie and Elaine handle most of the daily operations. Having a daughter and an aunt both named Irene, Rosita named the shop after the old standard Goodnight Irene. The four women have very different styles, which adds spice to the gifts and decorative accessories found here. They considered their own shopping desires when choosing the shop's inventory and looked for trendy, reasonably priced items they would want to find locally. Goodnight Irene showcases home and garden décor, wine, antique furniture and a room devoted to baby gifts. Plan your next treasure hunt at Goodnight Irene, where you can enjoy the advantages of big city shopping without the big city.

504 W Winnemucca Boulevard, Winnemucca NV
(775) 623-4661

Kathleen's

Two tastefully designed display windows draw you into Kathleen's, where shopping for women's clothing and accessories is the main attraction. "We are fashionable, not trendy," says owner Kathleen Stephens, who welcomes customers with a cheerful greeting. Visitors have remarked that she seems interested in your friendship first before your business, though the pride in what she does is certainly evident in the eye-catching displays that she has created to showcase the clothing, jewelry and countless accessories. Everything for a total look is here, and if you are not able to visit the shop, Kathleen can still assemble a wardrobe of style and grace for you. Indeed, personalized service for women who don't drive or can't get out is a specialty at Kathleen's. The owner generously provides meeting space for various local groups, including the Red Hat Society ladies, and is proud that her store is known as the place to meet and talk with local women about anything. Don't feel left out if you are a man. Kathleen treats her male visitors with characteristic graciousness, even providing them with a refreshment. When you drop by with your wife, you will probably find other husbands waiting and might make a few new friends. For a delightful shopping experience, visit Kathleen's.

18 N Main Street, Yerington NV
(775) 463-4455

Anacabe's– Elko General Merchandise

The longevity of Anacabe's–Elko General Merchandise can be attributed to founder Joe Anacabe, who firmly believed in offering quality products at an honest price. When Joe first opened in 1936, he sold mostly dry goods, groceries and other sundries and quickly gained a reputation for being friendly and fair. For more than 70 years the popular shop has been a community hub where locals gather to share news and stock up on the necessities of life. The store underwent remodeling shortly after WWII, and groceries were eliminated to make way for more outdoor supplies and clothing, including products from such companies as Filson, Carhartt and Whites. Anita, Joe's daughter, was raised above the store and felt it was her duty to return to the store to help her mother, Margaret, after both her father and her half-brother Frank passed away. Anita has been behind the counter for 30 years now and continues to offer the same friendly service and quality products that her customers and friends have come to count on. Her husband and town mayor, Mike Franzoia, and their children, Teresa, Andrea, Mateo and Kristina, are also frequently on hand, following in Joe's footsteps and offering great service to everyone who comes through the door. On top of that, the helpful and loyal staff will make sure you find what you need. Become part of an Elko shopping tradition and find everything you need for working and playing in the great outdoors at Anacabe's– Elko General Merchandise.

416 Idaho Street, Elko NV
(775) 738-3295

J. M. Capriola

J. M. Capriola, owned by Doug and Paula Wright, boasts an in-stock inventory of more than 400 different pieces of Western wear and gear intended for the working cowboy. The store features Garcia bits and spurs, first fashioned in the late 1800s by legendary cowboy gear craftsman G. S. Garcia. Joe Capriola, one of Garcia's apprentices, started his saddlery business in Elko in 1924 and opened J. M. Capriola in 1929. The company name remained the same through several ownership changes. In 1978, J. M. Capriola bought out the Garcia Bit and Spur Company. Today Capriola's bits and spurs are still made by Mexican craftsmen trained in the Garcia tradition and remain the only spurs and bits in the world that carry the Garcia name. This family-owned business has grown and the practice of suppling high-quality gear remains the same. The smell of wood and leather welcomes you inside the two-story shop with the red horse on the roof. Here you'll find handmade leather chaps and ladies who can guess your hat size just by looking. Capriola's displays a variety of Western wear, for working or playing, along with beautifully made boots and silver jewelry to complete an outfit. From saddles to shoo-flies, bridles to bits, everything you need for the Western lifestyle awaits your visit to J. M. Capriola.

500 Commercial Street, Elko NV
(775) 738-5816
www.capriolas.com

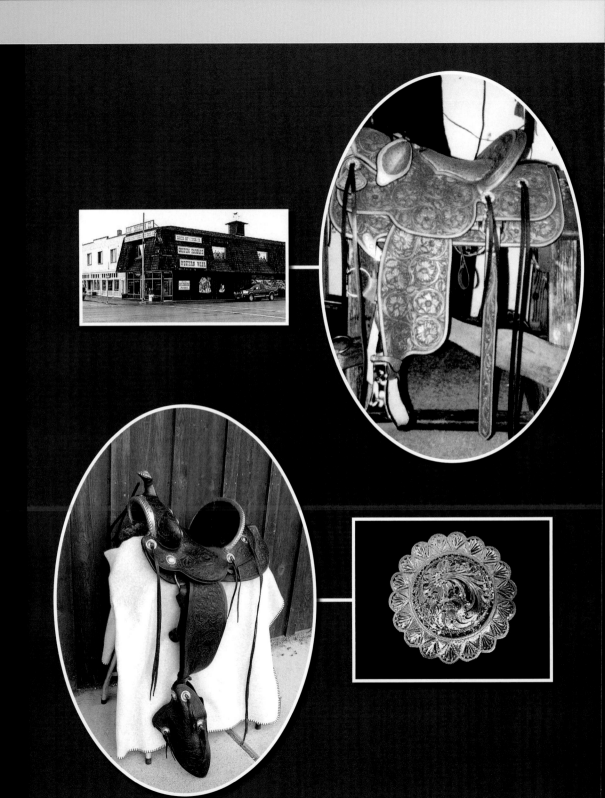

Flower Basket

Buying a creative flower arrangement in Ely is as simple as contacting the Flower Basket. This shop, where residents stop in for espresso, ice cream and gifts, as well as flowers, has been serving the community since 1952 with everything from prom corsages and wedding flowers to gifts that congratulate or offer sympathy. On most days, you'll find Maureen Vaught and her daughter Cricket at work. Many members of the family contribute their talents, along with several friendly employees. The Vaught family added the Espresso Depot to the Flower Basket in 1995 at their downtown location. Soon, the shop needed more space to accommodate the many coffee customers coming in for great espresso and the Flower Basket and Espresso Depot moved into its current location in East Ely. The building it calls home was built at the turn-of-the-last-century and has a colorful history. Stop in on your way to the Ghost Train of Old Ely and say hello, and pick up an espresso that many say is the best they have had in a long time.

445 E 11th Street, Ely NV
(775) 289-2828

Pahrump Valley Winery

"We always hear from visitors that this is like a desert oasis," says owner Bill Loken of Pahrump Valley Winery. That oasis in Pahrump quenches a visitor's thirst for award-winning wines, tours and fine food and drink at the on-site restaurant. Pahrump Valley Winery is the oldest and largest winery in the state and has won more than 100 national wine awards since opening in 1990—32 of them in 2006 alone. A small vineyard at the winery produces the grapes for about 1,500 bottles of Zinfandel. The rest of the grapes are brought in from various locations in California. Among the fine varieties you'll find here for tasting and purchase are the Desert Peak, made with the Pinot Grigio grape with hints of citrus and lemon and the sweet Desert Blush, with its hints of peach and apple. Visitors can tour the winery and see how the wine is made. "We want people to find it a pleasant diversion from all the crowds in Las Vegas," says Loken, who co-owns the winery with his wife, Gretchen. The winery hosts many events throughout the year, including a popular grape stomping festival in the fall. If you're looking for fine cuisine to go with your wine, you'll be delighted at the offerings of Symphony's, the on-site restaurant. Offering New American and Continental cuisine, the restaurant is Zagat-rated. Though it's just an hour outside Las Vegas, "visitors feel that they get a Napa experience in Pahrump," Bill says. Come to Pahrump Valley Winery for fine food, wine and fun events.

3810 Winery Road, Pahrump NV
(775) 751-7800 or (800) 368-9463
www.pahrumpwinery.com

White Pine Brewing Company

A thirsty visitor or Ely resident gets a delightful surprise upon entering White Pine Brewing Company, a company that has mastered the art and science of brewing. Steve MacMillan, co-owner and brewmaster, discovered a hop variety that's native to White Pine County while recreating in the great outdoors. He's had the hop tested for suitability and is growing it now for use in the brewing company's signature White Pine Harvest Ale. The company does not stop with brewing beer. It micro-ferments wines and meads, too. If coffee is your beverage of choice, you'll be deeply satisfied with White Pine coffee, micro-roasted on the premises from hand-selected green coffee beans. Steve is well known in Las Vegas brewing circles for his 20 years as a successful brewmaster and educator. He is an adjunct professor at the University of Nevada at Las Vegas, where he teaches a brewing sciences course, a coffee course and a summer program of beer education abroad. He's also a certified beer judge. In addition to Steve, Diane Kirby is co-owner and assistant brewmaster. Above all else, Steve and Diane want their brewery to support the community. They have set up a sister nonprofit business called Harvest Moon to raise substantial funds for community projects. Next time you are thirsty, taste a spirited beer or other fabulous beverage at White Pine Brewing Company.

617 Great Basin Boulevard, Ely NV
(775) 289-4555
www.whitepinebrewing.com

Index by Treasure

Index by City